To Cheri,
with Best
Wishes
Linda

Speculative Theology and Common-Sense Religion

Princeton Theological Monograph Series

K. C. Hanson, Charles M. Collier, and
D. Christopher Spinks, Series Editors

Recent volumes in the series

Kevin Twain Lowery
Salvaging Wesley's Agenda: A New Paradigm for Wesleyan Virtue Ethics

Ralph M. Wiltgen
The Founding of the Roman Catholic Church in Melanesia and Micronesia, 1850–1875

Ronald F. Satta
The Sacred Text: Biblical Authority in Nineteenth-Century America

Matthew J. Marohl
Faithfulness and the Purpose of Hebrews: A Social Identity Approach

D. Seiple and Frederick W. Weidmann, editors
Enigmas and Powers: Engaging the Work of Walter Wink for Classroom, Church, and World

Stanley D. Walters
Go Figure!: Figuration in Biblical Interpretation

Paul S. Chung
Martin Luther and Buddhism: Aesthetics of Suffering, Second Edition

Steven B. Sherman
Revitalizing Theological Epistemology: Holistic Evangelical Approaches to the Knowledge of God

David Hein
Geoffrey Fisher: Archbishop of Canterbury, 1945–1961

Speculative Theology and Common-Sense Religion

Mercersburg and the Conservative Roots of American Religion

Linden J. DeBie

☞PICKWICK *Publications* · Eugene, Oregon

SPECULATIVE THEOLOGY AND COMMON-SENSE RELIGION
Mercersburg and the Conservative Roots of American Religion

Princeton Theological Monograph Series 92

Copyright © 2008 Linden J. DeBie. All rights reserved. Except for brief quotations in critical articles or reviews, no part of this book may be reproduced in any manner without prior written permission from the publisher. Write: Permissions, Wipf and Stock Publishers, 199 W. 8th Ave., Suite 3, Eugene, OR 97401.

ISBN 13: 978-1-55635-476-2

Pickwick Publications
A Division of Wipf and Stock Publishers
199 W. 8th Ave., Suite 3
Eugene, OR 97401.

Cataloging-in-Publication data:

DeBie, Linden J.

Speculative theology and common-sense religion : Mercersburg and the conservative roots of American religion / Linden J. DeBie.

xiv + 116 p. ; 23 cm. Includes bibliographical references.

Princeton Theological Monograph Series 92

ISBN 13: 978-1-55635-476-2

1. Mercersburg theology. 2. Theology, Doctrine—United States—History—19th century. I. Title. II. Series.

BX9571 .D35 2008

Manufactured in the U.S.A.

*In memory of the Reverend Dr. Howard G. Hageman,
who introduced me to Mercersburg and to the Reverend Jeff Roth,
who nurtured its memory*

Contents

Introduction ix

1 Common-Sense Religion 1

2 Speculative Theology 31

3 Mercersburg and Princeton 57

Conclusion 105

Biblography 111

Introduction

THIS IS AN ESSAY IN AMERICAN RELIGIOUS THOUGHT. IT DESCRIBES THE way an improvised variation of German idealism was worked into the fabric of conservative, nineteenth-century American, Protestant religion, and clashed with conservative Protestantism's reigning philosophical informant of common-sense realism. The clash is described in terms of a controversy between theologians, pastors, and laity involved with the Mercersburg movement, but told from Mercersburg's perspective. Indeed, the clash intensified into a religious war of words, with both sides fearing for the future of Christendom unless their side prevailed.

A Cultural Framework

The precipitant "religious war" was a result of the times. The nineteenth century was an age of academic optimism—a time when confidence was high that simple and straightforward answers could be had to explain previously mysterious, natural, and social phenomenon. The post-Enlightenment's respecters of reason employed a scientific perspective. Expectations were that systems of thought be comprehensive, duplicating life and the world in prose. And when the answers or theories contradicted one another, further scrutiny was required. The result was a prevailing atmosphere of competition. The climate encouraged the ancient conviction among many that philosophical and scientific theories were mutually exclusive of one another. Rival systems were simply "wrong," and being wrong, likely dangerous. Progress was perceived in modifying or replacing obsolete systems with new systems based on better, more up-to-date, more scientific information.[1] Old systems resisted being replaced for a variety of reasons, with cultural reasons being just as significant as scientific reasons. For example, be-

1. For example, consider as earlier paradigms the philosophical systems of the Enlightenment, in Hobbes (1588–1679), Descartes (1596–1650), Locke (1632–1704), Spinoza (1632–1677), and Leibnitz (1646–1716).

ing thought wrong carried obvious social penalties: A thinker might be dismissed with the system. Indeed, such dismissals were common, as witnessed, for example, for this particular study, in the way that Kant's national recognition was eclipsed with the rise of Hegel's philosophy in Germany, with the same shared cultural sense of innovative advance witnessed later when automobiles replaced horse-drawn carriages.

The Enlightenment's scientific perspective carried with it a subtle dogma: the exclusivity of systems. Certainly there was some sense of how different systems might complement each other, but the age was marked by the search for scientific explanations for human experience. The West exhibited a fascination for comprehensive descriptions and unified theories. The expectation was that the best description would duplicate "real life," and so explain the world "as it is."[2]

By the turn of the century a more immediate concern intensified suspicions of wrong ideas and bad descriptions of reality. The British, Europeans, and Americans were disturbed and uncertain about the revolutions in France. In America this concern bordered on hysteria. Traditional Protestants felt the earth beneath beginning to give way:

> the leading thinkers of the American Calvinistic tradition experienced in acute terms the need for an apologetical philosophy. ... In America the need stemmed from a concrete situation: the religious decadence of the Revolutionary epoch and the fear, felt particularly in the post-war period, that French infidelity was engulfing the universities.[3]

The response seemed obvious, given the persuasion of the age. American Calvinists could either shore up their crumbling edifice, or they could build a new one. The leaders involved with the Mercersburg movement chose to do the latter. But they met with great opposition from those who would repristinate what they had.

What the American Calvinist tradition had, a little less than a century before the Civil War, as its primary philosophical informant, was realism.[4] The form of realism most influential in America was the

---

2. For a provocative critique of the Enlightenment (including some underlying and unconscious agendas, motives, and presuppositions of the seventeenth and eighteenth centuries) see Rorty, *Philosophy and the Mirror of Nature*.

3. Alhstrom, "Scottish Philosophy and American Theology," 261.

4. As a medieval doctrine in opposition to nominalism, realism held that universals exist objectively and outside ourselves. However, in modern philosophy, realism has

one that came from Scotland. It was the result of the initial efforts of a variety of philosophers, but most of the credit goes to Thomas Reid (1710–1796) and Dugald Stewart (1753–1828), and it initiated a period in which common-sense realism dominated America's educational institutions, most importantly for our study, beginning with the arrival of John Witherspoon at Princeton (1768).[5] Witherspoon brought common-sense realism with him to America, and his influence remained healthy even to the days when Mercersburg's rival contemporary, Charles Hodge, took control of Princeton. A key component attracting theologians and church leaders to realism and its Scottish offshoot was a consistent metaphysical dualism. For evangelicals, it was a philosophy that kept the worlds of nature and spirit "safely" apart. Princeton believed that the threat to this neat bifurcation of reality came from German idealism and its "mad scheme" to unite the worlds of flesh and spirit.

Mercersburg and the Movement

The duality so revered by American evangelicals was preserved in the host of influential American colleges. Almost as if it were a rearguard movement, the attack on this universally-held dogma came from an unlikely place. After all, when one thinks of great movements and clashes between erudite scholars, one usually thinks of urban, cultural centers—big universities with old colleges. This is not so with the Mercersburg movement. While Mercersburg is a town in Pennsylvania,

---

come to mean that material objects exist independently and outside our sense experience and ourselves. This was where it opposed idealism. Again, the more ancient idea of idealism was that reality was a product of reason or the mind. German idealism (as taught by Hegel) was actually a phenomenology or speculative science, which sought to extinguish the dualism inherent in both realism and idealism, but by finding its unity in Spirit (*Geist*) was still considered to be a form of idealism.

5. Witherspoon, *Lectures on Moral Philosophy*. Witherspoon was, at that time, a recent convert to Scottish realism. His older sources were Shaftsbury and Hutcheson. However, Reid was invoked and eventually relied upon to refute the findings of Hume—whom Witherspoon called an "infidel writer"—and so established the epistemological foundation of Princeton's philosophic thinking in common-sense realism. Witherspoon goes on to say that "in opposition to this [Hume], some late writers [Thomas Reid and James Beattie] have advanced, with great apparent reason, that there are certain first principles or dictates of common sense, which are either simple perceptions, or seen with intuitive evidence. These are the foundation of all reasoning, and without them, to reason is a word without meaning," 50. See also Noll, *Princeton Theology: 1812–1921*. The brackets with names are mine.

neither Philadelphia nor Pittsburgh plays a major role. Instead, one must envision endless rolling landscapes, a distance even from the more modest cities of Lancaster and Reading. Mercersburg is, to this day, a quiet farming community. Yet, that was where the German Reformed Church in America chose to move its seminary (academy) from its previous home in York, Pennsylvania (1836), and that is where the attack on common-sense realism was staged.[6]

At the head of the academy was the Mercersburg movement's founder, Frederick Augustus Rauch. Rauch, a German-born philologist, was the first to introduce Hegelian ideas to America, immediately setting off a controversy with his colleague at the seminary, Lewis Mayer.[7] Mayer was at home in the old dualistic tradition of Locke, Edwards, and Witherspoon. Soon an American Presbyterian, John Williamson Nevin, remarkable for his enthusiasm for all things German, joined Rauch on the faculty. With the premature death of Rauch, a Swiss-born scholar, Philip Schaff, joined Nevin in 1844.[8] Schaff's German education eminently qualified him to apply the newest ideas of Germany's mediating school to his historical inquiries. Rauch the philosopher, Nevin the theologian, and Schaff the historian—these three were the founders of the Mercersburg movement.

It was strange to these scholars that something as fashionable in Europe as idealism would be so unwelcome in America. When Schaff arrived from Germany and found Nevin hungry for the "new German learning," he must have thought him typical of America's educated elite. What a blow it was to discover Nevin the rare exception. Simply put,

---

6. Its first home was in Carlisle, Pennsylvania. It was moved from Carlisle to York in 1825.

7. For more on Rauch's Hegelian roots see DeBie, "Frederick Augustus Rauch: First American Hegelian," 70–77. For a different view, see Easton, *Hegel's First American Followers*. Easton and I have sparred over who was first to present Hegel's ideas to America. Easton acknowledges that Rauch taught and published before the Ohio Hegelians. However, his conviction that Rauch did not subscribe wholeheartedly to the Hegelian philosophical system excludes him from claim to the title "first American Hegelian." Yet, Rauch's system is so obviously charged with the Hegelian spirit and methodology that the fact that Rauch remained a churchman and an evangelical, unlike Hegel, hardly disqualifies him from the title "Hegelian."

8. Schaff's name underwent several changes in the process of being Anglicized. Originally it was spelled Philipp Schaf. Here citations will reflect the spelling when the cited work appeared.

Schaff and Nevin believed themselves to be "evangelical catholics"[9] importing the newest breakthroughs in theological science to the faithful in America.

If it were truly as simple as that, Mercersburg may not have encountered such resistance. Much of their heartache was the result of misunderstandings produced in the maelstrom of heated debate. Yet the biggest single source of philosophical rejection on the part of their detractors came as a result of America's failure to appreciate the adjustment made by the mediating school in Germany and by Mercersburg in America, to the so-called unorthodox systems of Hegel and Schleiermacher.

Mercersburg believed that the adjustments made by the mediating approach rendered it completely orthodox. In the wake of the waning influence first of Schleiermacher and then later of Hegel, a loose alliance of philosophers, historians, theologians, etc., sought to mediate a path between Christian "orthodoxy" and the idealism of Hegel, Schleiermacher, et al.—hence the name, "mediating school." Typically these scholars accepted the authority and reliability of Scripture, even as they approached Scripture critically and scientifically. Perhaps most significant for this study was their opposition to rationalism and the importance they placed on intuition in the process of knowing. Also crucial was their general acceptance of Hegel's speculative method in which history develops itself in a logical manner according to dialectical principles.

Nevertheless, Mercersburg's detractors never came to appreciate the subtleties of the mediating approach. Whether the problem was Mercersburg's poor communication (although Mercersburg would insist that they had made their case and made it clearly), or evangelical confusion over Germanic concepts, or, more likely, Mercersburg's alleged "softness on Rome," (i.e., their compatibility with the Roman Catholic Church), the failure resulted in open theological warfare.

Again, the supporters of both realism and idealism believed that orthodoxy was threatened by failed systems of philosophy, both felt an obligation to be scientific and comprehensive (if not systematic) in their description of the problem and the solution, and both felt there could be but one answer. The result was the controversy we describe.

9. Perhaps this term better than any other describes the character and thrust of the Mercersburg movement. However, in an age of rabid anti-Catholic sentiment, it was a brand that would contribute significantly to Mercersburg's opposition.

Common-Sense Religion

IN THE NINETEENTH CENTURY, MANY, ESPECIALLY THE MERCERSBURG school of teachers, considered Germany the preeminent and inspired source of artistic and scientific creativity. Germany's post-Enlightenment thinkers vied with one another, and with Great Britain and France, for a place in intellectual history, and their writings contributed enormously to Western development in politics, in education, and in the arts. Their influence on the Mercersburg movement was fundamental.

In our discussion of German philosophy (chapter 2), we go back only as far as Kant, whose reaction to the Scottish philosopher David Hume represents a watershed for Western philosophy. However, in identifying in German idealism an alternative to English empiricism, we anticipate the clash that would rage much later in America.

Still, in our discussion of Hume we need to come to terms with his philosophical predecessor, John Locke, who could be hailed as the founder of English empirical science.[1] He was revered among nineteenth-century, American evangelicals, many of whom considered him the father of modern philosophy and the unsurpassed apologist for Christian theology. In his forging of their beloved system, Locke supplied the reasoning that would later support their conservative religion.

---

1. Locke learned philosophy amid the Scholastic Aristotelianism of Oxford circa 1659, so his dualism was naturally a Greek inheritance. But he found no pleasure in what he believed was Scholasticism's trite and technical obscurity. His philosophic quest began with his reading of Descartes. Cartesian dualism or *ontological duality* provided much of the agenda of the period's philosophical speculations.

Locke and English Empiricism

American theologians, deeply influenced (if negatively affected) by the insights of empirical science, were reticent to stray from the good advice of Locke, Hume's forerunner.[2] Nor would they easily recover from Hume's skeptical lessons. Many believed his essays were an unprovoked diatribe and concluded that a system in which reason must rely on sense experience for certainty will leave nothing to believe in and little to know. Chagrined as they were, the doctrine acted on them like gravity on objects in space. Even while they would distance themselves from Hume's conclusions, they were drawn to an empirical perspective.

Perhaps circumstantially, Locke sustained what many believed was the natural cleavage inherent in reality: the enigma of mind and body. But a new preference was demanded within this ancient dyad. In the tension of thought and things, Locke made "sense certainty" the warden of speculative reason and the guardian of the world of spirit. His indebtedness to Descartes included inheriting his predecessor's fundamental presupposition: the duality of mind and body. In beginning with a two-tiered universe of mind and body, he continued the ancient Greek/Christian graft of religion and philosophy, where the term "spirit" became a philosophical trope for "things unseen" and where the term "flesh" would head the grouping of "things seen."

The list of dialectical oppositions that followed from this *ordo sacra* found parallels in the philosophical contrasts of reason and faith, finite and infinite, objective and subjective, and, as fundamental to our study, body and mind. Locke's contribution, in keeping with the age's growing fascination with empirical science, was to give the place of honor to "things seen," thereby supporting the shift of authority to claims made about the world verified by sense experience.

The increased role of sense verification in the philosophical discipline marked the shifting paradigm. For Locke, factual knowledge required interaction between the observer's mind and the object of perception (the thing to be known) by means of the idea. So, although he affirmed the reliability of common sense, satisfied that the world was

---

2. In respect to Hobbes it must be stated that he inaugurated the modern era with his empirical philosophy of mind. But Hobbes never achieved the popularity of Locke, nor was his *Leviathan* directed at the question of the mind and thinking. Unlike Locke, Hobbes was not systematic in his investigations, nor did he posses the dualism that Hume inherited from Locke. See Nidditch, "Foreword," viii–xi.

pretty much what it appeared to be, still, he believed that the ideas that entered one's mind were somewhat like pictures. He thought of them as copies of things and not as the things themselves. For Locke, the uniqueness of the idea and the object of perception created a duality within the perceptual process that prevented an encompassing identity from being created. The problem for Locke was that just such an identity was required in order to know the object as it really was.

Locke believed that what objects really were included an essence, which continued to be philosophy's proverbial "missing link." Without that link, or missing piece, the object remained partially hidden. This put religious and moral claims at considerable risk in the juxtaposition of reality's twin peaks of body and mind. As for the summit "body," claims unsupported by empirical methods were immediately suspect, especially the habit of citing sections of religious literature to substantiate facts about the world and how it works. As for the summit "mind," an absence of knowledge of the essences jeopardized any confidence in things like souls, which were commonly perceived as a complex essence of an individual being.

Strangely, Locke did not doubt the reality of essences, just that they could be known.[3] Perhaps a fine point, this lingering symptom of dualism allowed him to continue as a practicing (if highly unorthodox) Puritan. Locke was content that religious propositions need not be verified by scientific reason, which depended on sense experience. Rather, the believer must rely on special revelation for religious knowledge. In that respect Locke remained conservative, satisfied that the Christian Bible supplied what is necessary for spiritual understanding.[4]

Still Locke planted the seeds of doubt that took root in Hume's skepticism.[5] Hume drove the point home with frightening clarity. Compelled to discover how we know that our ideas about the world, especially our moral ideas, are reliable, he developed a critical approach that shared

---

3. "Truths belonging to Essences of Things, (that is, to abstract *Ideas*) are eternal, and are to be found out by the contemplation only of those Essences: as the Existence of Things is to be known only from Experience" (Locke, *Essay*, 562).

4. As argued in his *Reasonableness of Christianity* (1695) and his two defenses of Christianity (1695 and 1697).

5. "Unlike most men, who are more prone to believe than to doubt, Hume, a sceptic [*sic*] by temperament, found it more congenial to doubt than to believe. He was also a sceptic by philosophical conviction." See Mossner, "Introduction," 20. See also Miller, "Of scepticism with regard to the senses," section II, 238–39.

Locke's confidence in empiricism. Hume argued that knowledge rests on experience. Like Locke, the Scots philosopher remained confident that his method did not thwart common sense.[6] On the contrary, he believed his arguments were utterly practical. Rather, his targets were arguments born of passion and characterized by overstatement, the kind of arguments Hume found rampant in religion. But his skepticism went deeper than Locke's did.[7]

Hume chided the traditional philosophers with rhetorical questions he knew would not be satisfactorily answered. What does it mean to accept the hiddenness of an essence? Does its hiddenness make it immaterial? Likewise his answers, forcefully delivered with smug genius, changed the course of philosophy: "Of course not!" In fact, calling a thing immaterial is a tautology that makes it a substance. And calling a hidden thing a substance is a tautology that makes it immaterial. For something to be hidden it must have been revealed. Yet, what is being claimed for the essence is that it is not revealed. The conclusion for Hume was obvious. Calling a thing an essence is tantamount to predicating an immaterial substance. Such a predication is meaningless, and the idea of an "immaterial substance," is a conceptual oxymoron.[8]

Naturally the change wrought by Hume had implications for the field of philosophy and the course of Western intellectual development. This is certainly the case for Christian theology. The consequence of placing full confidence in the senses was additional stress on the model of a dualistic world. With credibility clearly on the side of "body," the weak link appeared to be on the side of "mind." Still, stripping the mind of divine qualities and reducing it to a functional role as a processor of ideas left much to be explained. If knowing is merely mental

---

6. Kant wrote in his famous defense of Hume, "I should think that Hume might fairly have laid as much claim to common sense as Beattie" (Mossner, "Introduction," 20).

7. Hume shared Locke's acceptance that ideas arise from experience, but Hume eschewed Locke's metaphysics. "We have therefore no idea of substance, distinct from that of a collection of particular qualities, or have we any other meaning when we either talk or reason concerning it." And, "The idea of a substance as well as that of a mode, is nothing but a collection of simple ideas" (*Human Nature*, 63).

8. "Every quality being a distinct thing from another, may be conceiv'd[sic] to exist apart, and may exist apart, not only from every other quality, but from that unintelligible chimera of a substance" (*Human Nature*, 271), and "These philosophers are the curious reasoners[sic] concerning the material or immaterial substance, in which they suppose our perceptions to inhere" (281).

process, then what initiates the ideas? What contains them, and the process? Hume came very close to rejecting an immaterial self behind a working mind. His declaration of the impossibility of having a sense-validated impression of the self seems, ostensibly, to be just that. Yet Hume couldn't shake Locke's fundamental description of the mind as a picturing mechanism that needs a background or slate, it needs something on which to be imaged.[9] Nor would he equate the brain with the mind, turning all into a physical process. He remained a dualist, proceeding as if his ideas were the product of an organic machine whose product (ideas) owned the mind, just as the mind owned the ideas. Mutual ownership implied a self, undeniably divided, yet essential. Hume appeared satisfied that his ideas, or findings, especially as derived from observation and common sense, were utterly reliable.

What Hume retained of Locke's philosophy of mind is of vital importance. The mind became a metaphorical slippery fish, hard to grasp out of the water (in abstraction), yet elusive in the water (as phenomenon). It remained an immaterial thing, yet it was neither substance nor essence. This raised a crucial question for a new generation of philosophers. How is it that the mind receives representations of real things in the world, without itself being a real thing in the world? In light of this, it is not entirely surprising (while still granting the genius required) that Hume's skepticism provoked Kant to postulate a "transcendent mind."

Meanwhile, another eminent Scottish philosopher, Thomas Reid, was reeling from the revelations of Hume. Reid believed that Hume discounted too much of what constituted knowledge.[10] He felt that in

---

9. Locke states his concept quite clearly, "Let us then suppose the Mind to be, as we say, white Paper, void of all Characters, without any *Ideas*" (Nidditch, *Locke's Essay*, 104). Hume in contrast says, "Having found such contradictions and difficulties in every system concerning external objects, and in the idea of matter, which we fancy so clear and determinate, we shall naturally expect still greater difficulties and contradictions in every hypothesis concerning our internal perceptions, and the nature of the mind, which we are apt to imagine so much more obscure, and uncertain" (*Human Understanding*, 280–81). However, it remains the mind that receives the impressions, and instead of a "White paper," Hume calls the mind "a kind of theatre" (301).

10. Later Reid's reaction was intensified by an exchange between the philosophers resulting from Hume's tepid comments about Reid's *An Inquiry into the Human Mind on the Principles of Common Sense* (1764). In reply Reid admitted that Hume's system raised within him serious objections to commonly held principles, but in his "Dedication" Reid wrote, Hume's is "a system of skepticism[sic], which leaves no

Hume's legitimate respect for the limits of knowledge, he placed too much confidence in the theory of ideas. Like those he would criticize, Reid believed in a world divided into mind and body. But, for Reid, the dilemma was knowing, not how we know. Reid would not overly abstract the process, not to the degree of Hume, and certainly not to the exclusion of practical knowledge (common sense).

The tradition of Locke and Hume had all standing or falling on the concept of a picturing, processing mind. Reid suggested that Hume's error occurred with the concept of "idea" as the mediator of what was outside the body. Obviously, charged Reid, the idea itself could not be tested. It could not be determined to what degree the idea conformed to the object of perception. Reid felt that by addressing the problem in terms of how the process occurs in the mind, Hume ignored common sense. Reid insisted that common sense dictates that the things in nature are given to the mind as the image of the things themselves. He concluded that the real problem was with Hume's concept of the idea as it occurs in the mind. It wasn't the existence of mind that troubled Reid, but the question of Hume's theory of the idea.

Reid pressed Hume to explain what proof exists that the idea corresponds to the object of perception? None, asserted Reid, because there is no way to isolate an idea and examine it as an idea. In fact, as far as Reid was concerned, the assumption is that the idea is pretty much the object of perception itself as pictured in the mind. So why predicate the idea? Why can't the mind have an immediate and unmediated experience of the object itself? After all, concluded Reid, that is exactly what perception offers and that is what experience and common sense reveal.

In Reid, American common-sense realists of the early nineteenth century found their answer to the formidable criticisms against Locke (most especially Hume's). The school of Scottish common-sense philosophy was widely perceived by American philosophers, scientists, and divines as the philosophy that restored Locke to his place of intellectual preeminence.

---

ground to believe any one thing rather than its contrary." See Reid, *An Inquiry Into the Human Mind, On the Principles of Common Sense*, v.

The American Calvinists

Reid became the philosophical champion of Americans in the Reformed family of faith. Scottish Protestants were largely Presbyterians and adherents of the theology of John Calvin chiefly by influence of his friend and colleague, John Knox.[11] Anglicans had a strong connection to Calvinistic theology as evidenced by the Lambeth Articles.[12] Dutch and German Reformed people leaned most heavily on the Heidelberg Catechism, which is fundamentally a Calvinistic document.[13] Puritans and Separatists—indeed, Protestants of every stripe—had something of Calvin to be both grateful for and to contend with.

One issue of contention was over what was more and more being perceived as an outdated philosophical foundation. The Scottish and English had long since turned to Shaftesbury, Butler, and Hutcheson[14] for their apologetic, and ultimately many of them (including the most influential evangelicals in America) laid claim to Reid and Stewart. But another important contention—fomenting in the American experiment itself—was with Calvin's ecclesiology, especially in the European assumption that church and state were closely tied together, and that the state owes allegiance to the church.[15] America provided the first

---

11. John Knox (c. 1513–1572) was a Scottish theologian of enormous influence. He met Calvin in 1554 in Geneva before serving the English refugees as pastor in Frankfurt. T. H. L. Parker writes: "His [Calvin's] influence in Scotland, immense as it was, was nevertheless still not direct but mediated through his personal relationship with Knox in Geneva and through his writings." *John Calvin: A Biography*, 144.

12. Nine theological propositions compiled at the conferences in Lambeth, England, in 1595, of a heavily Calvinistic flavor.

13. Research over the last three decades points to the eclectic nature of Ursinus's Heidelberg Catechism. Several scholars have ferreted out the sources of the Catechism and shown them to include Melanchthon, Laski, and Bucer, among others. But in the end, John Calvin is its primary source, certainly when it comes to its eucharistic doctrine.

14. Anthony Ashley Schaftesbury (1671–1713), Joseph Butler (1692–1752), Francis Hutcheson (1694–1746), all of whom today are more recognized for their moral philosophy than for their epistemology.

15. Calvin was intent on limiting the secular authority of the church, to be sure. But he understood church authority in terms of spiritual and moral oversight, and in this regard the church was autonomous and above the state. Likewise as spiritual and moral concerns were tied to one's ultimate salvation, the church's authority was primary and not separated from secular authority, but merely distinguished from secular authority. Calvin wrote, "For the magistrate, if he is godly, will not want to exempt himself from the common subjection of God's children. It is by no means the last significant part of this

testing ground of voluntary religion and thus forced an overhaul of even the more democratically structured polities of the Reformed, Congregational, and Presbyterian congregations. But America's commitment to voluntary religion (disestablishment) unfolded gradually. From the earliest days, denominations vigorously vied for official recognition. When it appeared that a competing denomination might gain recognition, opposing confessions rallied to seek religious disestablishment.

During the Revolutionary period, the Baptists and Presbyterians fought against Anglican establishment. They even included within their ranks a "freedom of religion movement," which gained support in Virginia. In 1777, thanks to the political efforts of George Mason and James Madison, Virginia suspended the payment of tithes to the Church of England, which was the most likely candidate for establishment at the time.

Thomas Jefferson was perhaps the principal politician advocating religious freedom and with it the disestablishment of religion in America. His efforts were monumental in the ratification of disestablishment bills. Pennsylvania disestablished itself in 1776 and other states followed, but it took Massachusetts until 1833 to ratify disestablishment.

It would be naïve to think that disestablishment came quickly and easily to North America. Prior to the Revolutionary period, it was believed by many that the government's established religion would regulate philosophical inquiry, and so it was assumed that the reigning confession would curb impious thinkers as much as it would discipline heretics. The assumption was that the church would underwrite the nation's philosophy just as it had in Europe. Voluntary religion changed all that.

The separation of church and state in America made the domination of confessions in political life much less significant than in Europe, and, ultimately, relatively insignificant. Likely this encouraged a philosophical independence that we now recognize as inevitable. As time went by, philosophy was divorced from theology. Still, while the European experience of state-sponsored religion was conspicuously

---

for him to subject himself to the church, which judges according to God's Word—so far ought he to be from setting that judgment aside!" McNeill, *Calvin: Institutes*, 1216. And although "Christ's spiritual Kingdom and the civil jurisdiction are things completely distinct . . . civil government has as its appointed end, so long as *we live* among men, to cherish and protect the outward worship of God" (*Institutes*, 1486–87).

absent in America, its remnant remained, and the idea that intelligent, philosophically astute religious leaders would influence the affairs of state persisted.

Even as late as 1800, most Americans hadn't shaken the view that the state requires religious direction. Schaff's own analogy was that the state requires religion, as much as a person's will requires a conscience.[16] America's leaders of the colonial period never assumed that the country would be governed outside of a religious context, and the majority of Revolutionary era leaders felt the same way. (Jefferson might be an arguable exception, but the rare one at that.[17]) However, during and following the Revolutionary era, leaders began to believe that the free and uncensored exchange of religious views, within an independent church setting, could insure and even enhance orthodoxy. Such exchange, while not resulting in the enormous political control that state sponsorship of religion assured in Europe, would still carry weight.

That weight would eventually become diffuse as it spread between the dozens and dozens of religious entities, which could now seek recognition. Yet, until the middle of the nineteenth century, American political and religious life was guided by a relatively small number of denominations. They were primarily a combination of Reformed or Presbyterian confessions. This was so with the majority of settlers from Scotland and the Protestants from Ireland, and the English Episcopalians, to a varying degree. Protestant Germans were generally either Reformed or Lutheran. The Congregationalists, many of whose churches had been in America the longest, had a venerable association with Reformed theology, especially through the influence of the Mathers, Cotton and Increase.

In North America, as in Europe, religious leaders were listened to! Americans participated in voluntary religion. They went to church, they read religious journals, they followed the changes in theology and denominational practice, and they argued about who was "right."

16. Philip Schaff wrote, "Church and state are equally necessary, and as inseparable as soul and body, and yet as distinct as soul and body." See his *Church and State In the United States*, 10. The book is essentially a defense of voluntary religion in America, and regards the passive but essential role of religion in America superior to that of ancient and modern European models.

17. This has been popularly argued by a number of historians. Jefferson was a convinced deist, and there were others who shared his views. However, the majority of Americans and their leaders, held more "orthodox" views.

Religion was important to them, and so was politics. Each influenced the other.[18] But in America, the influence, thorough as it was, was passive. So, while official recognition of a denomination or theology by the state was unconstitutional, influence was freely applied, and influence was an important concern of religious leaders.

America also shared Europe's recent "Awakening." Not the same one, of course. America had its own brand of neopietism, inspired by the New England preachers. That began in 1740, and Jonathan Edwards was its most famous influence. Another Awakening, in 1800, spread the New England theology to the South and West.[19]

Edwards infused his Westminster Calvinism with a piety that stressed personal conviction of sin, conversion, and individual moral responsibility. But Edwards's theology had its base in English empiricism. At Yale, Edwards read Locke, and Locke unfolded to Edwards a vista of two worlds; of two great tiers of knowledge, naturally opposed and ontologically distinct. Rarely were they brought together, and then,

---

18. A controversial but powerful study verifying these facts can be found in Gaustad, *Faith of Our Fathers*.

19. Ascribing a date to such a universal phenomenon as the Great Awakening is unsound except to offer the reader a temporal context. The history of the revivals that shaped so much of early American history is long and detailed, and the terms associated with these revivals can be confusing. Commonly, the effects of these religious movements were contained in the names "Old Side" and "New Side," "Old Light" and "New Light," and "Old School" and "New School." The *New Light* perspective had become universal among American Calvinists by the early nineteenth century. *Old Side* practice had virtually disappeared. The *New Light* challenge dates as far back as the late 1600s, but is most commonly associated with the Great Awakening. It is broadly described as a form of pietism having both European and American characteristics. The *New Light* revolution began as early as 1690 among the Dutch Reformed, and centered on identification with certain leaders' particular interpretations of Calvin, and spilled over into social practices including, among *Old Siders*, long hair (as preferred to short by *New Siders*), more personal freedom (especially on Sunday), and an obvious class distinction (with *Old Siders* being the wealthier class). *Old Siders* kept closer ties to Europe and were generally less progressive and less willing to follow the latest fashions. As time went on another modernizing movement appeared called *New Light*. Gifted preachers supported the *New Light* cause as typified in enthusiastic preaching, an emphasis on inner conversion, and rigid standards for admission to the Lord's Table. Such preaching became the hallmark of The Great Awakening and can be most closely identified with Theodorus Jacobus Frelinghuysen (c. 1726) among the Dutch, Jonathan Edwards and George Whitefield (c. 1746) in New England, and Samuel Davies (c. 1748) in the South. A second great religious movement began at the end of the eighteenth century. Its roots are in New England, but it spread throughout American Protestantism.

only by divine intervention. Locke's writings taught Edwards that there was a natural world and a moral world. Empirical science was the key to the first. Moral science unlocked the second.

Each world was guided by its own set of intractable, universal laws. Just as nature was infused with obligation to the laws of science, moral science insisted that each individual conscience was equipped with a sense of right and wrong.[20] Pointing to individual responsibility was significant for the American experience. Each member of society had inalienable human rights but also inescapable social responsibilities. Failure to live according to moral law could not be excused by an appeal to ignorance. The laws were written on each individual's moral conscience and, therefore, could not be ignored. Neither could sin be simply excused.[21]

The Defense of Realism

American realists were in general agreement that an innate mental faculty provided knowledge of the unseen world of moral obligation. This Lockean legacy was vital to the philosophy sweeping America in the wake of Edward's decline and during the rise of the second Great Awakening. By the 1800's Scottish common-sense realism had entrenched itself at most American colleges. Timothy Dwight, at Yale, found it suited his traditional Calvinism. Its congeniality with science and science's recent discoveries brought a welcomed change, allowing philosophers and theologians alike to soften the doctrines of providence and election made harsh by scholasticism.

Harvard was headquarters to the Unitarian movement. Unitarians prized the notion of moral obligation, and their leaders found the work

20. This development is the legacy of Locke's student, Shaftesbury. Locke might be characterized as answering the ultimate question of what constitutes right behavior by saying that, "Right behavior is doing what God told us to do." But Edwards recognizes a moral faculty in men and women. Here we can readily see that Edwards, while deeply steeped in Locke, hadn't concluded his studies with Locke. Like other American evangelicals, Edwards supplemented Locke's rigorous empiricism with the work of the British moralists.

21. Jonathan Edwards was himself an original philosopher whose new apologetic borrowed from the sentimental theories of Schaftesbury (*The Moralist*). His argument is forcefully presented in his debate with Chauncy (see his *Treatise On the Religious Affection*, published in 1746). Harry S. Stout has an excellent description of this in his chapter on the "Awakening," in *The New England Soul*.

of the moral philosophers, Reid and Stewart, invaluable. Indeed, the notion led them to conclude that all people are endowed with the quality of basic human goodness.

Samuel Johnson's Berkeleyan stronghold of King's College (Columbia) was stormed by the forces of empiricism and became a citadel of Scottish philosophy. The empirical sciences offered proof of a real, material universe. For the progressives on the faculty, it was the proof they needed to dispel the chimera of Berkeley's "immaterialism" and free the college from the posthumous ideological grip of the great bishop.

At Andover Seminary, where Edwards A. Park remained the last New England defender of the traditions of Locke and Edwards, a great perception of malaise appeared. The findings of science were rocking orthodoxy, and it occurred to Park that the old fortress might need shoring up. Park shared with the majority of religious leaders in America the conviction that support would come from the wonderfully practical and thoroughly orthodox teachings of Reid and Stewart.

However, long before common-sense realism became America's preferred intellectual perspective, John Witherspoon had imported his own version of common-sense philosophy to Princeton College (1768). Witherspoon adapted the Scottish philosophers to harmonize his Westminster confession.[22] His success testifies to the welcoming richness of the American experience. Intellectuals and practitioners alike celebrated common-sense realism's eminently practical outlook. The opening of the new frontier seemed to favor a rugged independence in individuals who would face great odds "taming the West." That rugged

22. As previously reported it was Witherspoon who first imported Scottish common-sense realism to Princeton (see Witherspoon's *Lectures*). Sydney Ahlstrom was one of the first modern historians to identify Witherspoon as an early source of Scottish realism in America. Ahlstrom called Witherspoon the "first real ambassador" of Reid and the Scottish school. Under Witherspoon Berkeley fell to the Scottish school with the rest of American institutions following suit. Of course, Witherspoon had his own way of reading the Scottish philosophy. Says Ahlstrom, Witherspoon's "common sense" was mediated by his "Evangelical bias." See Ahlstrom, "The Scottish Philosophy" 261. See also Noll, *The Princeton Theology* and Hoeveler, *James Mc Cosh and the Scottish Intellectual Tradition*. Witherspoon's first dependence in moral philosophy was Francis Hutcheson (1694–1746). Thomas Reid's impact was only recently felt by Witherspoon who included him in his bibliography and Stewart had a major influence on Charles Hodge, Princeton Seminary's great teacher and leader, and the most popular critic of the Mercersburg movement. Witherspoon wrote, in opposition to Hume, that Locke had uncovered the principles of philosophical reasoning, without which philosophy is pointless (*Moral Philosophy*, 50).

individualism, sought as much by intellectual pioneers as by settlers, would be lionized in the presidency of Andrew Jackson (1829).[23] The shared standard was accepting the world as it is, and there was virtue in taking things at face value. No wonder a philosophy that assured its adherents that the world was pretty much as it appeared would gain support.

Princeton continued to represent the tradition of Witherspoon, and the insights of Locke, Reid, and Stewart remained the girders of Protestant orthodoxy's revitalized Calvinism. That remained the case, however, with diminishing enthusiasm, with Princeton's legendary leaders after Witherspoon, Archibald Alexander and Charles Hodge. Hodge had it in his head that even Andover had wavered in its orthodoxy, that the conservative tradition was in jeopardy, and that he and Princeton were the last defenders of the legacy of Locke and Edwards.[24]

Princeton was predisposed to be suspicious of any new ideas brought from abroad. As frightening as was the prospect of facing the future with a rigid and outdated Calvinism, more frightening was the prospect of what Europe offered. Revolution after revolution shook Western civilization, and with each new twist of leadership, there arose a new threat to orthodoxy, brandishing its philosophical justification. Deism, agnosticism, and the "horror" of materialism marked the European context in the minds of many American religious leaders.[25] Religious periodicals recorded the writers' frightened, emotional reactions as frequently as they recorded their more measured reactions. Effectively and mistakenly, Americans equated German idealism with German rationalism, and thus with all that seemed to unsettle Europe.

---

23. It has been argued that the Mercersburg movement was, in part, a reaction to Jacksonian democracy. Nichols suggests as much in Nichols, *Romanticism In American Theology*, 260.

24. That Hodge was distinguished as America's patron of orthodoxy is widely known. Less well known is the fact that Hodge inherited the role from his teachers, certainly Alexander, but even more from Samuel Miller. Miller was the faculty historian. It was Miller who established Princeton's reputation as a besieged bastion of orthodoxy and the last home of scholastic theology, and it was Miller who initiated the contest with the emerging theology of New England (Nichols, *Romanticism*, 16.)

25. As previously cited, Sydney Ahlstrom's "The Scottish Philosophy and American Theology" includes a description of the extent of American anxiety about Continental excesses.

In 1839 the *Biblical Repertory and Princeton Review*[26] summarized the view of American religious leaders: With the death of Brown,[27] in 1820, the world lost the last champion of the Scottish cause. Since then, metaphysics in England ground to a halt. Yet this came as no surprise to the Princeton writers. In spite of their enthusiasm for "Scottish thought," the Princeton faculty criticized what they believed to be the inherent weakness in the "reactionary" philosophy of Reid and Stewart, and in the pages of the *Princeton Review* they lamented the common-sense philosophy's "skeptical bent" that seemed to them to betray an uneasy defensiveness. The editor concluded that, such obvious parochialism would never develop the positive impetus needed to address the challenge of "transcendentalism" nor curb the growing liberal direction of American Protestantism.

However, the Princeton thinkers offered no immediate solution to the problem of transcendentalism, nor were they ready to replace or modify common-sense philosophy. Indeed, they acknowledged their debt by crediting Brown with the able defense of the faith. Still, they argued that the American situation was unique, in that much of the disturbing trends that plagued Europe were absent in America. That was, they said, until recently.

The *Princeton Review* concluded that, for years, America blossomed under the tutelage of Locke and Edwards, "the greatest of modern

---

26. The *Biblical Repertory and Princeton Review* began its life in 1825 as the *Biblical Repertory: A Collection of Tracts in Biblical Literature* by Charles Hodge. It remained in the control of Hodge virtually the whole of his life. Hodge's son, Alexander, reported in his biography of his father that *The British Quarterly*, the oldest quarterly in the US at the time (1871), wrote of *The Biblical Repertory and Princeton Review* calling it the "greatest purely theological Review that has ever been published in the English tongue." At the same time, Dr. Lyman Beecher called *The Biblical Repertory* "the most powerful organ in the Land" (Hodge, *The Life of Charles Hodge*, 257).

27. The authors refer to Thomas Brown (1778–1802), a student of Stewart and successor to the chair of moral philosophy at Edinburgh. Ironically, Brown was by no means a simple clone of his teacher and departed from the Scottish school at several junctures. Specifically, his criticism of Hume was more mature in its understanding of Hume, which made his arguments stronger. Still, his popularity at Princeton was based on his traditional theism. Brown assured confidence when he wrote in his *Lectures on the Philosophy of the Human Mind*, #73, III, 533, "We know, then, in this sense, why our mind has been so constituted as to have these emotions; and our inquiry leads us, as all other inquires ultimately lead us, to the provident goodness of him by whom we were made." Even more interesting, for this study, was the decidedly empiricist direction taken by Brown.

Christian metaphysicians." But lately, from Europe and at the hands of the New Englanders—Dwight, Hopkins, and Taylor[28]—the floodgates of heresy were opened wide. Sadly, they repined, no great American philosopher appeared to take philosophy to a higher metaphysical level. The result landed the orthodox at the mercy of the Germans and worse, Princeton charged, at the mercy of the second-class mimics of the Germans, the French and English and a few misguided Americans.

The transcendentalism spoken of by the Princeton authors was German idealism, or what they believe were idealism's prodigal offspring in idealism's various European and American manifestations, such as Cousin, Coleridge, and Emerson. The charge by Princeton was quite basic: German thought was simply too esoteric for American minds. Concealed within that esoteric "nonsense" was a tempting appeal that was nothing less than heresy. It was latter-day Gnosticism, the suggestion that within the vision created by an excited imagination there existed some special truth found nowhere else. With a mocking sneer, Princeton satirized that, naturally this private awareness need not bother with the ordinary pursuit of truth, nor need it recognize the time-honored and rigorous methods brought by British philosophy and science. They concluded:

> there are certain limits to intellectual powers, which the immortal Locke endeavored to ascertain, and beyond which we float in the region of midnight, so those who have forgotten these cautions have in their most original speculations only reproduced the delirium of other times, which in the cycle of opinion has come back upon us like a phantasma [sic] or a hideous dream.[29]

In contrast, *The Princeton Review* recognized America's hunger for a practical philosophy, one that would support and encourage the building of a country. It so happened that at the point that America would be building, science offered the necessary technical assistance. The industrial revolution and the breakthroughs in science provided a synergism unparalleled in history and the marriage of convenience between Scottish common-sense realism and Baconian empirical

---

28. All of whom were considered together by Princeton as New Light leaders and revivalists.

29. Alexander and Dod, "Transcendentalism," rev. of *Elements of Psychology* and "An Address delivered before the Senior Class in Divinity College," 88.

reasoning gave intellectual credibility to the schemes of the ambitious young republic.[30]

Originally, virtually all systems of thought were imports to America from the Continent and Great Britain. Early on, Berkeley's popularity in Europe made him popular in America. Likewise, the thinking of Locke was appropriated by Edwards to give backbone to his evangelical aspirations. For most evangelicals, Scottish realism was merely a clarification of Locke's "self-evident" principles.[31] At the crux of it all was realism's separation of the worlds of sense and spirit, and from the tidy compartmentalizing of the world into separate but compatible spheres, the evangelicals at Princeton sought to reconstruct their conservative system of theology.

The Worlds of Sense and Spirit

Locke's division of the mind into a collection of mental faculties would factor significantly into a growingly empirical philosophical perspective, and Newtonian visions of stable laws determining and predicting the outcomes of physical events fulfilled the realists' expectations in the laboratory. The view grew into a dogma: thinking must mirror nature,[32] and an appropriate paradigm encompassing them both would reflect the mechanical nature of the physical world. Mental faculties would be understood according to their function.

The Scottish philosophers set about adjusting Locke's findings, arguing that while the mind should be understood as a complex mechanism, and while it might be abstracted according to its functions (faculties), whose jobs are to receive and organize information, the mind remains self-identical. The abstractions are in relation to the various functions.

This was an important insight in the answer that the orthodox would give to Hume's assaults. Skeptics were reminded that, in the moral

---

30. This becomes especially prominent in the popular Jacksonian democracy movement. But the "manifest destiny" dreams of Americans developed earlier. For an excellent study of this phenomenon see Bozeman, *Protestants in An Age of Science*.

31. Generally, this was the view of conservative evangelicals in America. We noted it in Witherspoon, but Hodge and his followers treated Locke with a respect bordering on devotion.

32. See Rorty's chapter on "Our Glassy Essence" in his *Philosophy and the Mirror of Nature*.

sphere, the common-sense understanding of this "self-evident unity of experience" provided confidence that the universal laws of right behavior were available to each thinking individual. People are obligated to respond to an essentially moral universe, just as they understand and so must respond, to an obviously law-abiding universe. The value of reason is displayed in cooperation with common sense. Rational beings appropriate the laws of the universe that come to us through experience by applying them to their science, their art and culture, as well as their religion and morality. Likewise, rational beings recognize the limits of experience placed on them by their senses. Transcendence of those limits is not only irrational, it is impossible!

Nineteenth-century America, just like its parent Europe, abounded with practical "evidences" and "natural theologies," and analogies for the existence of God found easy publication.[33] Arguments that addressed skeptics' questions about the claims of revelation and the seemingly counter-claims of, for example, geologists, were sharpened and rehearsed among educated believers. As a result, many American Calvinists came to express themselves from an increasingly empiricist and certainly anthropomorphic starting point, especially when speaking apologetically, as well as when articulating the subtleties of their ethical convictions. The new anthropomorphic center of knowledge encompassed nearly all of evangelical expression. From Edwards on, the knowledge of self preceded the knowledge of God.

The mind as starting point kept the question of the mind high on the philosophers' agendas. Realism is obliged to locate consciousness either physiologically, in regions of the brain, or in mental phenomena, abstracting from the mind its various functions.[34] Still, location of

33. Surely William Paley (1734–1805) was a fundamental source of much of this thinking. His *The Principles of Moral and Political Philosophy* (1785), *Horae Palinae* (1790), and especially his less original but widely read *View of Evidences of Christianity* (1794) and *Natural Theology* (1802) popularized this way of thinking, such that developing elaborate proofs of God's work in nature came to dominate many approaches to theology. While Paley borrowed broadly from Abraham Tucker, Paley's prose and presentation captured the attention of the reading public. The analogies of design were already popular in America. These "proofs" were considered evidence of a law-abiding universe, created by a benevolent if distant God. Such thinking clearly marks the American framers of the Constitution. For more on deism's influence on the early American presidents and statesmen see the previous citation of Gaustad, *Faith of Our Fathers*.

34. This was a central characteristic of the faculty psychology practiced at Princeton.

thought seemed mandatory. As the mechanistic age transformed society, and machines became futuristic symbols of an orderly, controllable, and understandable process, nature and mind required a new, modern comparison. The comparison became pervasive: mind and nature were like machines, and the metaphoric umbrella that covered them both was "mechanism."

Realism at Princeton

James I. Good, the most verbose critic of Mercersburg, published a book discrediting the movement, charging them with idealism, and warning evangelicals of the deceptive metaphor that would replace "life as mechanism" with "life as organism."[35] Although Good got carried away with a laughable but popular racial argument about English-speakers and their inability to comprehend German reasoning, his assessment of American tastes in philosophy was right on track. He observed that Americans were realistic dualists, primarily interested in practical questions of sense experience.

Good's provincialism tolerated Rauch, for the foreigner he was, but he hated Nevin for betraying his native world-view. Rauch, he said, was a German, and so it was understandable that he would scorn the world of sense, the phenomenal world as he called it, and pursue what his culture believed was the real world of ideas. But, said Good, Nevin should have known better. His dismal attempt to import German thinking to a Scots-Irish mind only produced drivel.

At least Good was fair to grant the German-educated Rauch a German perspective. Other American evangelicals were not so generous. Princeton admired Rauch for his reputation and his churchmanship, but they were united in rejecting the premise of his philosophy: his deep-seated monism, his rejection of Locke and Stewart, and the pomposity of the romantic delusion that made all German idealists pantheists.

In spite of Princeton's avowed conservative traditionalism, they shared with Mercersburg a modern perspective: they both began an-

---

35. Good was a second-generation critic of Mercersburg growing up in an anti-Mercersburg household. Clearly his criticisms were deeply biased. Still, his proximity to the controversy and his exhaustive study of it make him essential reading. Here Good applies terminology that dramatically captures the thrust of the debate.

thropomorphically. But their resulting psychologies were worlds apart, indeed, two worlds apart. Princeton's metaphysics had absorbed the teachings of the Scottish school, and authors have described its celebrated acceptance at Princeton.[36] Sydney Ahlstrom was instrumental in recording Princeton's use of a Scottish informed, metaphysical dualism to reconcile—but not unite—the worlds of matter and spirit. All the while, in Mercersburg's mind, the latent skepticism found in dualism continued to brazen mankind's ignorance of the spiritual world, while merely whimpering at the common-sense, literal acceptance of the material world.

Not perturbed by skepticism's threat, the orthodox theists at Princeton enshrined traditional beliefs by deifying the doctrines themselves. It was a solid defense against both scrutiny and criticism. They believed what earlier Protestants believed God had revealed. Princeton's theological texts included Turretin, the great Calvinist scholastic (as stiff a dogmatist as they come) and John Dick.[37] Witherspoon and Edwards were revered, as was Locke. The Scots were respected for the aid they gave to well-reasoned faith. Dualism, as it had informed the New England tradition, was believed, virtually without question (even if its components were in need of periodic adjustment), and the

---

36. As previously cited see Ahlstrom, "The Scottish Philosophy," and Noll, *The Princeton Theology*.

37. Alexander read to his students from Francois Turretini's (1623–1687), *Institutio Theoligiae Elenchicae* (Geneva, 1679–1685). Turretin was a major source of the federal theology that brought about the dominance of scholastic Calvinism. Turretin's *Institutes* continued as Princeton's chief text in theology, even though it was in Latin. From Princeton's perspective, there simply was nothing better in English, and while Hodge harbored differences with Turretin, for most of the thirty-eight years that he met with both the second year and senior students, he assigned readings from Turretin. It remained the text until 1848 when Hodge replaced it with his own *Systematic Theology*. However, records indicate that another Princeton textbook in use was the one by John Dick, *Lectures On Theology*, 2 vols. (Edinburgh, 1834). It was a popular theology among evangelicals, and Nevin used it at Mercersburg as his principle text (even though Nevin criticized Dick for his rationalistic bent). His students' notes track his frequent departures from Dick, and his fundamental philosophical disagreement with the author: that the mind receives knowledge as if it were a blank slate. For Nevin, this resulted in the error of understanding "knowing" as if the mind encounters its subject from the position of pure objectivity. Nevin's classroom lectures were published in Reading by I. M. Beaver in 1913 and edited by William H. Erb under the title *Dr. Nevin's Theology: Based On Manuscript Class-Room Lectures*. The above citation appears on 57–58.

conservative citadel of tradition appeared relatively safe, if somewhat alone and harassed.

The only perceived threat to Princeton and Old School orthodoxy in America was initially thought to be home-grown. Revival theology, the new American Arminianism[38] prescribed by Finneyites and assorted others, was American-born and considered, by Princeton, of serious consequence. But Princeton believed revivalism could not rival rationalism for the harm it could do to "true religion." In rationalism, the world confronted the blight of deism and pantheism, and the poisoned apples of rationalism's witchcraft: political revolution and the spread of Roman Catholicism. Their single comfort was that this threat was from abroad. Hodge went so far as to visit Germany for a first-hand look.[39]

The later shock that came to Princeton was finding the scourge of rationalism at their doorstep, along with a host of unwelcome, idealist-inspired positions. Only several miles from "the last bastion of orthodoxy" at Princeton, the Mercersburg movement was accused of inviting

---

38. Referring to Jacobus Arminius (Jakob Hermans, 1560–1609), the anti-Calvinist. By this time the epithet "Arminian" was attached to Reformed theologies that were perceived as Pelagian, that is, teaching that individuals can take the initial and important steps towards salvation before the experience of divine grace. In this American context, revival theologies sustained a free will in individuals, which is able to make a choice in accepting Jesus as Savior. However, oftentimes the nuances of these doctrines were lost on the fundamental and biblically simple positions of what was often called "New Measures" theology. Perhaps the most significant and well-documented case is that of Albert Barnes, where Barnes's defense in the face of accusations that he did not teach according to the federalist doctrines of Scripture, was that, since Scripture doesn't say that the guilt of Adam was imputed to his offspring, Barnes would not teach it. Said Barnes, Scripture merely says that human beings are sinful through Adam, and that was all that he would believe and teach. For a fascinating study of how this controversy exposed the rift between Old School thinking and the increasing biblical literalism of the New School, see Stansbury, *Trial of Albert Barnes*.

39. Ostensibly Hodge went to Germany to study languages. His weakness in Greek was a special problem. He hoped to meet and study with some of Europe's greatest minds, spending half his time in France and the other half in Germany. The French stay didn't work out and so Hodge spent his time in Germany, and he kept a journal that revealed the intense suspicions harbored by him and his Princeton colleagues about German learning and speculative theology, which they confused with earlier rationalism. In Alexander's letters to Hodge, he wrote of his concern, warning Hodge of the "poisen[sic] of neology!" and predicting that the German speculative air that he breaths will "either have a deleterious effect on your moral constitution, or else . . . your spiritual health will be confirmed." Hodge's journal makes insightful reading and was published in his son's biography, *The Life of Charles Hodge*.

a threat far worse than misguided revivalism. Princeton was convinced that German idealism carried within it the utter demoralization of the Protestant faith in America, and now Mercersburg was idealism's pawn. As early as the writings of Rauch, James Alexander of Princeton warned of Germany's incompatibility with American thinking. He argued in various articles in the *Princeton Review* that the barriers preventing commerce between the two were dualism and America's common-sense realism.

In his review of Rauch's *Psychology*, Alexander maintained that Stewart coined America's philosophical vernacular. Said Alexander, It's not that Rauch hasn't the right to express himself differently. Granted, the Scottish metaphysical "phraseology" had certain "limitations." Still, the German system, which united the traditionally separate mental activities of will and reason into an organic unity of mind, was simplistic and led to the heresy of pantheism.[40]

Realism and Evangelical Theology

Naturally Rauch clashed head-on with reigning realism. Not long after his arrival he published a work describing ecumenical relations in Germany and commended the progress of the Reformed and Lutherans in unifying under one banner. He mistakenly referred to the Lutheran doctrine of the Lord's Supper as "transubstantiation."[41] The angry response by the writer that appeared in the *Lutheran Observer* was sterner than Rauch's error warranted. There was a great deal more behind the article than simply the reminder that the old Lutheran doctrine was called "consubstantiation."[42] The anonymous writer's rebuke included a strange renunciation of the Lutheran teaching on the Lord's Supper; strange in that "consubstantiation" was condemned as "magical"

---

40. Alexander was kinder to Rauch than might be expected, considering the contempt Princeton held for the "new German learning." Princeton's high regard for Rauch stemmed from his reputation as a pious churchman. The review was published in *Biblical Repository and Princeton Review* under the title "Rauch's Psychology."

41. Relating to the theology of the Eucharist, transubstantiation was the Roman Catholic view that the elements converted to Christ's actual body and blood, and that only the appearance (accidents) remained that of bread and wine.

42. Again, relating to the theology of the Eucharist and in opposition to the theology of transubstantiation, consubstantiation was the doctrine of Martin Luther, in which the actual body and blood of Christ co-existed with the substances of bread and wine.

superstition, and a doctrine "never given wide acceptance by Lutherans." Indeed, claimed the writer, Lutherans had always held to a Zwinglian view of the Supper, where no mingling of the sensual world with the spiritual occurs.[43]

Evangelical dualists were firm about the limits of spiritual experience. God was surely present, but exclusively through the mediation of the Holy Spirit. The Spirit was the bridge between the two worlds. Indeed, that was precisely the Spirit's operation (*opera ad extra*): to communicate the holy to the profane. This position accounts for the popular nineteenth-century evangelical doctrine of divine inspiration. It was generally agreed that God was present in God's Word, the Bible, but again, only by action of the Holy Spirit. Holy Writ was transcribed by men, but dictated by the Spirit. In effect, the Bible existed supernaturally in heaven before all time, and was communicated by the Spirit to the biblical writers.[44] Time and again, in evangelical doctrine after doctrine, the worlds of heaven and earth were forced apart and held distinct, except through the exclusive intervention of the Spirit.

When Nevin went a step further in what was already perceived as a Roman Catholic direction and lifted the Apostles' Creed to a status close (some would argue "quite nearly equal") to the place held by Scripture, John Proudfit,[45] an evangelical leader in the Dutch Reformed Church,

---

43. The anonymous attack was the work of Kurtz the *Observer's* editor. The controversy is covered on the pages of, *The Weekly Messenger of the German Reformed Church*, under the title, "German Characteristics" 1 (New Series), Nos. 19 (1835), 23 (1836), 27 (1836), 30 (1836), 35 (1836), 39 (1836).

44. Ironically, it is a doctrine that amounts to divine dictation, and as such, is virtually identical to the Roman Catholic doctrine of verbal inspiration.

45. John Proudfit was professor of theology at the country's oldest (with Andover) seminary in New Brunswick, New Jersey (originally Queen's College, now on the campus of Rutgers University). Antagonism between Proudfit and Nevin developed over Nevin's interpretation of the Catechism. Proudfit led the way in distancing the Dutch Reformed from her sister denomination. As accusations against Mercersburg within the German Reformed Church led to trials and divisions, the Dutch Reformed Church (Reformed Church in America) sided against Mercersburg and suspended all correspondence in 1852 with the following resolution: "*Resolved* that this Synod do hereby express in the most decided and unequivocal manner their protest against all these sentiments of a Romanizing character and tendency which are technically known as *Mercersburg Theology* as being essential departures from the faith, as calculated to lead yet further astray from the old landmarks of truth and to undermine the great principles of Reformation from Popery (E. T. Corwin, *Digest of Constitutional and Synodical Legislation of the Reformed Church in America*, 1906). This development was

protested and invoked the doctrine of divine inspiration to give exclusive place to Scripture above the Creed. Unlike the Creed, said Proudfit, the Bible is "revealed" truth. For his evidence, he cited the work of John Locke (*The Reasonableness of Christianity*), where the Spirit's mediation of the unseen world was "proven." Proudfit wrote, anyone can interpret Scripture, if the Spirit intervenes, and that "to apprehend and imbibe that heavenly light [Scripture] requires only the open eye of the soul ... by the operation of the Holy Spirit."

Even where the ancient Church had confessed the presence of Christ within the believer, mediation and confirmation by the Spirit were a nineteenth-century evangelical prerequisite. Mercersburg was insistent that union with God required union with the "human nature of Christ." The scandal of merger between the opposing worlds of sense and spirit provoked Jacob Helfenstein, a German Reformed pastor and leader of the denomination, to attribute Mercersburg's position to their tendency toward "Roman Catholic superstition." He called it the "vain speculations" of the German philosophy, and he marveled that Mercersburg could be so unaware that Stewart had since dispelled such fantasy.[46]

Evangelical suspicion of any divine object existing in the profane world was especially acute when it came to the objects of worship. Icons were adulterous. Liturgical forms inhibited the free working of the Spirit. Set prayers were surely insincere, since they were not the spontaneous moving of the Spirit. Only with "inward worship," where

---

especially dismal, since the two denominations had just celebrated their triennial together in Harrisburg, Pennsylvania, just eight years earlier, with John W. Nevin preaching before the assembly on August 8. Nevin's later complaint against the interference of the Dutch in the affairs of the Germans is recorded in his, "The Dutch Crusade." For a brief summary of this controversy, see my "Truce in the Dutch Crusade."

46. Jacob Helfenstein was the leader of the pro-revivalist forces in the German Reformed Church. He was the minister of the Germantown, Pennsylvania, church. Helfenstein was well known in the denomination for elevating the role of profession of faith and regeneration above that of the Heidelberg Catechism, thus provoking controversy. He chaired the judicatory (The Classis of Philadelphia) that heard and sustained the complaint of the Mercersburg theology in 1845. That year he took the complaint to the Synod in York, Pennsylvania, where it was dismissed. For Helfenstein's viewpoint see, "The Rule of Faith," and, "The Mercersburg Controversy." The series of events surrounding this controversy (all of which stemmed from Schaff's *Principle of Protestantism*) is wonderfully described in Donald E. Harpster's unpublished dissertation, "Controversy in the German Reformed Church in Pennsylvania With Emphasis On Nineteenth-Century Philadelphia."

a natural condition exists for the cooperation of will and spirit; only inwardly, do men and women experience the divine and benefit from its influence. Views to the contrary were considered to be Roman Catholic in nature.

No other hatred by evangelicals aroused such support as hatred of the Roman Catholic Church. Mercersburg's idealism became the target of this popular hatred at two levels. The speculative philosophy's attack on dualism required the full participation of the supernatural in the natural. Many evangelicals simply identified that as superstition, and they were used to thinking of Rome as the "mother of superstition." Often critics of Mercersburg simply assumed that their supernaturalism was another form of Puseyism, or, surely, Roman Catholic inspired.

Secondly, idealists in Europe were often at the forefront of the nineteenth-century ecumenical movement,[47] where attempts at dialogue and compromise were common. The obvious mediating tenor of the Mercersburg movement suggested the same compromising nature, and their various books and articles insisted that sectarianism and not Roman Catholicism, was the source of America's religious plight.[48] But anti-Roman Catholic sentiment was gaining intensity in America. Indeed, so virulent was the antagonism, that sporadic anti-Roman Catholic riots rocked American cities during the period of the Mercersburg campaign.[49]

New School evangelicals were becoming used to success. Their numbers were growing rapidly. More and more, they approved of revivals, spoke of their faith in terms of personal relationship with Jesus

---

47. Nineteenth-century American ecumenism really amounted to the cooperative efforts of the various denominations and Christian associations. These included a massive Sunday school movement, prison reform, temperance and abolition movements, and vast missionary societies. The effort effectively changed the face of Protestant America. However, in terms of bringing denominations into common confession and recognition of mutual ministries (i.e., what today we usually understand as the goal of ecumenism), that simply didn't occur in America. That was not the case in Europe.

48. This was a central thesis of Nevin's, "Pseudo-Protestantism." It was also a theme of Schaff's *Principle of Protestantism*.

49. Clearly the hostility was exacerbated (but by no means excused) by the magnitude of immigration. For example, Catholics increased from 200,000 in 1829 to 1.7 million in 1850. Nevin and Schaff were first-hand witnesses to the violence, with Philadelphia being the scene of several anti-Catholic riots. Nativism sought justification and power in the founding of what became known as the Know-Nothing Party (1840's–1850's), a political platform expressly hostile to Roman Catholics.

Christ, placed supreme emphasis on the Bible, and participated in the cooperative social and missionary ventures between denominations. They tended to embrace the Jacksonian ideal, and they identified their numerical success in proselytizing with the future success of the republic.[50] Commercial growth and development were seen to be signs of the Spirit's presence and approval. Science was tolerated for the advancement it provided, even though its claims seemed to chip away at "revealed" beliefs about the physical world. A stubborn love/hate relationship was forged, where, for example, the idea became popular that the "problem" of the discovery of dinosaur bones could be explained by arguing that God simply planted those bones to "test our faith." The growing antagonism between science and religion became a national preoccupation, ultimately leading, in the next century, to the sensational Scopes trial (1925), where a noted and powerful politician squared off with a renowned lawyer to prove, in popular opinion, the case of religion over science.[51]

Still, evangelical leaders, both Old and New School, could not remain oblivious to the questions raised by industrial society. The challenge of deism, materialism and empiricism needed to be addressed. The solid philosophical base provided by Locke and Edwards and the Scottish school begged for modern support.

Before Nevin ceased to be a practicing Puritan in the Old School tradition and embraced German idealism, he wrestled with these very

50. Even today this remains very much a part of what is called "evangelicalism" and the politically active "religious right." Prior to 1850 the various splinter religious groups neither considered themselves Reformed nor evangelical. They stemmed primarily from Puritan influence and revival preaching. They were opposed to a creed and preferred individual freedom in biblical interpretation. But when an association was formed around similar concerns and shared missionary efforts, the name they took (after the Civil War) was the Evangelical Alliance. This encouraged a new use of the term "evangelical" to what is common today. The preoccupation with numerical success and with adapting to the American cultural environment is strategically developed in Mark Noll's, "Evangelicals and Reformed; two streams, one source" and, "What Has Wheaton To Do With Jerusalem: lessons from evangelicals for the Reformed." It is interesting, as well as revealing, that Noll takes Mercersburg directly to task as the historical source of Protestant mainstream hostility toward evangelical philosophy.

51. The trial was held in Dayton, Tennessee (July 10–21, 1925). John Scopes was tried and convicted of teaching evolution contrary to a state law enacted on March 21, 1925. The famous evangelical (fundamentalist) and presidential candidate, William Jennings Bryan, led the prosecution. Scopes was defended by the celebrated trial lawyers, Clarence Darrow and Dudley Field Malone.

issues, and sought to reconcile himself to the changing face of faith as a modern evangelical. Traditionally, American Calvinists, with their European counterparts, made God's sovereignty a cardinal tenet. But the doctrine of divine sovereignty festered in what had long been a wound among Protestants: the doctrine of election. Sovereignty and the concomitant divine quality of omnipotence seemed to require absolute certainty of future events; not merely foreknowledge of future events, but the certainty that all future events are predestined. That clashed with an increasingly popular doctrine of free-will.

Common sense and evangelical piety convinced Nevin and a growing number of Protestants that freedom of choice is a fact of life. Common sense convinced them that religious truth needs to be tested according to individual experience. That anthropomorphic center brought psychology into the limelight. Replacing the post-medieval, Calvinistic psychology with a modern psychology was key to understanding the adjustments made by realists and idealists alike.[52] Realists would inventory revealed truth and conceive its entrance into the world in a way analogous to, but not ontologically the same as, a natural event. They argued that the mind is presented with revelation as with any mental phenomenon. Like the earlier Edwards, the conscience was then free to evaluate and appropriate that which was presented to it.

Confirmation of right religious knowledge was essentially left up to the individual, since justification was a psychological state often referred to as a "feeling." This is in stark contrast to the Calvinistic notion of justification as a religious fact, established by one's election. With the onus on the individual, it was no longer a question of God encountering the individual, but of the individual encountering God.

Perhaps the foremost spokesperson for the evangelical faith in nineteenth-century America was Charles Hodge. Hodge led Princeton in its battle against Mercersburg, and in that struggle Hodge articulated the heart and soul of conservative, American evangelical religion.

Hodge was a modern Lockean, schooled in the Scottish philosophy, and a convinced realist who considered all descriptions of intangible things as merely abstractions and without substance or being in the

---

52. The idea of considering Mercersburg in terms of the way it replaced the Reformed confession's primitive Calvinistic psychology with a new, organic perspective was the thesis of Nathan D. Mitchell's Ph.D. dissertation, "Church, Eucharist, and Liturgical Reform at Mercersburg: 1843–1857."

natural world. Still, Hodge shared with his fellow evangelicals a concern that American faith was in jeopardy because of the collapse of Lockean-style metaphysics in Europe. He therefore set about to publish his own system in an attempt to account for the faith in the midst of the confusion of the modern age. He vaguely alluded to his undeveloped and as then yet unpublished system, referring to it as "Realistic Dualism."[53]

The theological war between Nevin and Hodge may have delayed the publication of his system until 1865, where, in "Nature of Man," the outline of "dualistic realism" is laid out. (For no apparent reason, Hodge reversed the two words in his system's title.) "Life," writes Hodge, "is a predicable." Essences do not predicate being. Subjects predicate being. The idea of life derives from an abstraction on the essence of living things. Only "real substance" gives discrete particulars their identity, and only objective existence constitutes genus or species.[54]

In Hodge's ongoing struggle with Mercersburg (primarily Nevin), he would outline his theology. A cardinal tenet was the mediating role of the Holy Spirit, conducting the exchange between the seen and unseen. The salvific benefits of faith enter the world by divine decree issuing from the omniscient mind of God, and exist sublimely, apart from the real world, in a sphere of grace. Christian life is analogous to leaving the world of flesh and living in the world of spirit. Except that no one really leaves the world. Instead the Spirit imparts that world to individual Christian souls, giving them access to heaven when they die.[55]

---

53. In reality this may just have been a threat by Hodge, as a result of desperation. Hodge was well aware of the fact that he was not a philosopher, but no one had come forward to accept the mantle of philosophic leadership. His system's epistemological foundation resulted from his own re-working of the Lockean, Edwardsian, and Scottish systems, as is evident in his *Systematic Theology* (3 vols., 1871–1873). This off-handed proposal is recorded in his "Princeton Review and Cousin's Philosophy," and, as a diatribe, it raises serious questions as to whether realistic dualism would ever appear as a system in itself. In fact, it did not, except, perhaps, as the philosophic foundation of his *Systematics*.

54. See Hodge's "Nature of Man."

55. This credo and what follows in the next two paragraphs are a summary of what constitutes one of American religious history's greatest literary debates. The debate originally appeared throughout the summer months of 1848 in *The Weekly Messenger of the German Reformed Church*. It was inspired by a belated review of Nevin's *The Mystical Presence* by Charles Hodge. Hodge wrote the review at the request of Nevin's opponents and those who questioned the book's premise. Nevin had shocked his American Protestant readers by supporting Schaff's claim in his *Principle of Protestantism* that Protestantism developed in reaction to Roman Catholic authority.

Hodge concluded that the eternity of the Word precludes any change on its part. There is no evolution of doctrine. Rather individuals mature into a better understanding of the Bible's unchanging truth. Nor does the church evolve or change, that is, the "true church." Certainly the historic, "visible" church is mired in change and fleshly corruption, as evidenced in the Middle Ages, but the true church, says Hodge, is a gift of God, existing invisibly in the spiritual bond of its members.

Hodge's outline effectively articulates the theological template of the nineteenth-century evangelical mind. Throughout America, Protestants were taught to understand religion as the rational appropriation of "divine truth." The institutional fellowship created by the communion of the "inspired elect" was the church. Its role is the support of the saints. Its existence mirrors the intangible heavenly sphere where dwell all the saintly souls, and nowhere could this fundamental belief be more evident than in the common, nineteenth-century conviction that Protestantism was the recovery of original Christianity.

Even among the most educated Protestant leaders, the Protestant church system was believed to be the recovery of the religion founded by Christ, as it existed at the time immediately following the apostles.[56] This view supported the popular argument that Protestants were preserving

---

Using the original historical sources, Nevin demonstrated that the Reformation was a product of Roman Catholicism. He concluded that the historic confession of Reformed Protestantism, along with its Eucharistic theology, was essentially Catholic in character. Perhaps his most startling discovery was that, contrary to modern evangelical opinion, Calvin sustained the real presence of Christ in the Holy Communion. Hodge's rebuttal originally appeared as a response to *The Mystical Presence* in *The Biblical Repertory and Princeton Review* under the title, "Doctrine Of the Reformed Church, On the Lord's Supper." Nevin turned the matter into a debate by printing Hodge's entire review in the *Messenger*. Above each point made by Hodge, Nevin assigned a heading, and then followed each of those sections with his own, contrary argument. Step by step he sought to discredit Hodge's view, and tried to show how Hodge's conclusions were based on faulty historical assumptions, mis-interpretations, ignorance of the ancient sources, and, ultimately, Nevin's own work.

56. To some extent, this can be explained by America's, as opposed to Germany's, woefully inadequate historical science. Sensible leaders were likely to accept the common understanding of events without proof to the contrary. That the American Protestant church was a recovery of original Christianity was just too tempting a conclusion to question, and when its support appeared in a theory that certain early Protestant groups were actually a hidden remnant that resurfaced during the Reformation, even brilliant thinkers like Horace Bushnell and the eloquent layman of the Dutch Reformed Church, Taylor Lewis, were taken in.

the true church from Roman Catholic corruption. The glaring lacuna was historical proof, a painful fact of historical science in nineteenth-century America. The shared assumption among evangelicals was of a post-apostolic golden age that looked suspiciously like the loose confederation of evangelical denominations in nineteenth-century America. The unity of the early church was believed to be the shared activity of the Holy Spirit in their midst. Its polity was democratic and without any formal hierarchy. Its basis of belief was biblical, and the core of its doctrine complete.

Support for this outrageous claim came in the form of a spurious historical argument embraced by Hodge and the host of evangelical writers opposed to the Mercersburg movement. The theory held that immediately following the post-apostolic age, in an abrupt wrenching of church polity, certain corrupt leaders, like Cyprian, gained control and established, virtually overnight, the episcopacy and the hierarchy of Rome. However, in 177 AD, Polycarp and a band of refugees fled Roman persecution and settled in the Alps. There, orthodoxy remained unchanged and perfect, descending pristine, through a refugee migration during the twelfth century under the leadership of Peter Waldo.[57]

---

57. The theory appears in various forms and references in the religious periodicals of the time. The likely source of the theory is the Waldenses themselves. It was corroborated by sympathetic if naïve early Protestant historians. James Hastings Nichols (*Romanticism*, 43) suggests that Americans were exposed to the theory by Joseph Mede (1586–1683), whose apocalyptic interpretations mythologized what little factual base American historical science had. The past and future dispensations of the world were described in his *Clavis Apocalyptica* (1627), his discourses, and his *The Apostasy of the Latter Times* (1641). There were several interpretations of this theory, the least likely being that St. Paul founded the Waldensian community on his way to Spain. After that was the version that had Polycarp leading the community to safety in the Alps. More likely, the Waldenses were an offshoot of the earlier Albigenses "heresy." Their leader was Peter Waldo (actually Valdes, who died around 1205–1218). They did, however, lead the way in some of the earliest teachings of the Reformation, and they were in dialogue with several Reformation leaders. Schaff may have been the first historian in America to debunk the theory that the Reformation is traceable through some remnant, original community. His *Principle of Protestantism* identifies the Waldenses, the Hussites, plus other groups and individuals, as playing a crucial role in what would become the Reformation, but he is explicit in saying that these movements, among others, developed from within and in reaction to, Roman Catholicism. In addition, he writes, "We go farther however, and affirm, that *the entire Catholic Church as such, so far as it might be considered the legitimate bearer of the Christian faith and life*, pressed with inward necessary impulse towards Protestantism" (47). The insistence is on the natural, organic evolution of the church, in opposition to the theory that the Reformation

Throughout America this myth had gained wide acceptance among Protestants. The belief was that the true Christian Church remained underground and hidden for a thousand years, preserved from Roman Catholic corruption by the Waldenses, Albigenses, Henricians, and Paulicians, until the end of this so-called "Babylonian captivity"[58] brought by the Reformation.

Whenever and wherever the supernatural world of spirit might appear to share substance with the corporeal world of common experience, Princeton pursued a conservative path and insisted that the barrier (i.e., their highly prized, evangelical philosophical position of dualism) be raised. It was a benevolent dictatorship, concerned with preserving the interests of rational religion and the public good. It was a peaceful blockade, for the preservation and good of both worlds! Yet Mercersburg found it ill-conceived, fostering an inauthentic and unhistorical Christianity, and preventing the "real" union between Christ and believer.

---

simply recovered original Christianity, or that its impetus came from a hidden and pure source of Christianity. For a discussion of how this myth figured into the debate between Hodge and Nevin see my "Real Presence or Real Absence?"

58. The term originally refers to the ancient captivity of the Jews under king Nebuchadnezzar (604–562 BC). Later it was used in an allegorical sense, describing first, the exile of the Popes (1309–1377), then, and in the sense we have it here, by Luther, referring to the "slavery" of the church under Roman "superstition." Especially among many evangelicals in America, Roman Catholicism was viewed as the "anti-Christ." They suspected that Rome sought to control American politics, and would do so through the established Roman Catholic Church in the United States. Some evangelicals saw the United States as the "New Jerusalem," precisely because it was essentially Protestant and hostile to Roman Catholicism.

2

Speculative Theology

THE SWEEPING CHANGES OCCURRING IN GERMANY IN THE WAKE OF THE idealist revolution created an environment rich in ideas and choices. Most dramatic was the choice of which idealist to identify with, or in what direction to take him. By 1820 Schleiermacher's influence was on the wane, and in early anticipation of the declining influence of Hegel's philosophy, the Prussian minister of religion sought to return the ministry and the nation to a conservative, evangelical faith supported by a sympathetic philosophy.[1] In the years that followed, the next generation of idealist thinkers busied themselves answering the questions left by their mentors. Their answers took them in a variety of new directions, oftentimes away from their teachers. Still, their work remained characteristically idealistic. What is most enlightening for this study is the way the new idealists parted company over the question of dualism.

Kant's Revolution

Immanuel Kant (1724–1804) was of enormous importance to philosophy in general and to Mercersburg specifically. Mercersburg considered his idealism and his "dualistic system" of remarkable genius. With others, Mercersburg recognized that Kant had sustained the bifurcation of reality inherent in Hume and Western tradition, but had turned that tradition on its head.

Kant believed that rigorous skepticism of the kind promoted by Hume encouraged a type of rational knowing that believes only what it sees, smells, touches, feels, hears or tastes. With Kant, Mercersburg embraced the criticism of Hume that such rigor makes even the

---

1. Hegel had become a target of the growing evangelical (pietistic) movement.

simplest connections between events problematic. For example, seeing the sun come up today can never lead one to say (with the same factual certainty) that the sun will come up tomorrow. Hume's logic seemed inescapable: While seeing is believing, anticipating cannot carry the same factual weight. Nor will a fact of nature and experience provide provable platitudes of moral behavior.

Hume's challenge was devastating for ethicists who would be scientists. He led the way in a type of thinking that suggested that while we should "do to others as we would have done to us," we cannot *prove* it. Hume's point was that no matter how many empirical "facts" were produced to support a moral case, the *proof* must fail.

Hume demonstrated that an empirical science of ethics was untenable given the absence of the connection between events. Hume argued that common sense suggested that events follow in sequence. But, he continued, we go a step beyond common sense when we make a law of that experience, suggesting, for example, that the law of cause and effect determines the sequence. Hume found no evidence of such a causal "necessity." Nor is there physical evidence of universal moral laws that would make appropriate social behavior necessary. The facts of nature simply do not warrant such a conclusion.

Kant didn't disagree, he turned things around. For Kant, knowing wasn't simply a natural phenomenon. That is, our knowledge of the world wasn't exclusively the product of images in our minds. Surely the world of nature was real and existed outside our experience of it. That was to say, we don't dream the world.[2] But Kant insisted that we do think the world. The process included more than our reception of sense impressions. The mind was not, as Hume suggested, passive. The mind imposes something of its own on the objects of perception; it contributes something to the experience of knowing. While the things that compose the natural world offer themselves as objects of perception,

2. Kant aimed this caveat at Berkeley, "When I say that the intuition of outer objects and the self-intuition of the mind alike represent the objects and the mind, in space and time, as they affect our sense, that is, as they appear, I do not mean to say that these objects are a mere *illusion*." And, a bit further in the section he made it clear to whom he referred: "—we cannot blame the good Berkeley for degrading bodies to mere illusion." And again, "[Berkeley] maintains that space, with all the things of which it is the inseparable condition, is something which is in itself impossible; and he therefore regards the things in space as merely imaginary entities." See Kant, *Critique of Pure Reason*, 88, 89, 244.

the mind contributes the conditions that make perception possible, specifically context and sequence, space and time.[3]

The important qualification was the active role of the mind and the hidden quality of the objects it perceives. Kant believed that while the objects are as they are perceived (there is no deception), the objects are, after all, abstractions and not the things themselves.

The result of Kant's new philosophy was a redefinition of "Mind" as it operated in the world of nature and experience. He was no less a dualist, yet he defended the active, as opposed to the passive, role of mind in knowing, and so (I believe intentionally) he refortified the importance of the "unseen" in experience. He opened the door, again, to thoughts about the infinite, God, and the soul, all by postulating the existence of the "transcendent mind." For Kant, the mind initiates knowing, but the mind is its end as well.[4]

Kant's unique view from the twin summits of mind and body stimulated a new approach to the question of knowing, one of essential importance to Mercersburg. Given the reliability of the senses for validating experience, the question was raised: Are there other faculties that can validate other orders of facts? Later, Kant became aware of the looming problem of a world split into ontological opposites. This problem would occupy Kant in his later years as well as the next generation of German idealists.[5] However, Kant never shied away from placing his first confidence in the seen things of the world of body as the

---

3. This is the premise of Kant's first *Critique*.

4. "Since, however, in the relation of the given object to the subject, such properties depend upon the mode of intuition of the subject, this object as *appearance* is to be distinguished from itself as object *in itself*" (*Critique of Pure Reason*, 88). The object of which no experience is possible was a far cry from other intangibles like God and the human soul, because, unlike God, the object could be observed. Still, Kant was paving the way to renewed discussion of the unseen world of Christian faith: "This discussion as to the positive advantage of critical principles of pure reason can be similarly developed in regard to the concept of God and of the *simple nature* of the *soul*" (29). Indeed, Kant elaborated at great length in his famous second *Critique* (*The Critique of Practical Reason*) and in *Religion within the Limits of Reason Alone*.

5. Kant's third *Critique*, *The Critique of Judgment*, has been described as that—an attempt to establish the unity of experience separated by theoretical and practical reason. In his section number ninety-one, Kant states that a comparison of the structures of the two critiques "correctly occasion the expectation of being able someday to bring into one view the unity of the entire pure rational faculty (both theoretical and practical) and of being able to derive everything from one principle."

foundation of reason and in scientific support of a corresponding logic. And in reaction to the perceived impoverishment of the world of "mind" left by Hume, Kant discovered, in sense experience, the grounds for an equally valid, if not empirical logic of mind. Such a logic led him to defend the phenomenon of a "transcendent mind," and all that could be legitimately salvaged for belief in the world beyond the senses.[6]

The discussion reopened by Kant was pivotal for Mercersburg. A direct line of theological speculation can be drawn from Kant to Mercersburg, with Nevin engaging Kant in Nevin's most philosophical essays.[7] In reaction to Kant, Fichte, Schelling, Hegel, and Schleiermacher, the Mercersburg trio most identified with the later, German mediating school of theologians in their attempt to make the speculative science less antagonistic to Christianity. Nevertheless, all of the mediators were, to a great extent, the intellectual descendants of Kant.[8] These were the practitioners of the speculative method. They shared many differing views about philosophy and theology, and their divergent ideas of the church went from the new and radical idea of seeing it as a necessary social institution ("an arm of the state") to the traditional "belief" in the church as the means by which God would redeem creation.

---

6. "I have therefore found it necessary to deny *knowledge*, in order to make room for *faith*" (first *Critique*, 29).

7. Nevin writes, "This is what Kant makes so much account of, in his philosophy, as the *autonomy* of the will. The idea is one of vast importance, notwithstanding the great abuse which has been made of it in his school. The will, in its very nature, must be autonomic in order that it may be free; that is, it must be a law to itself, in such sense that its activity shall be purely and strictly its own in opposition to the thought of everything like compulsion exerted upon it from abroad." See Nevin, "Human Freedom and A Plea for Philosophy: Two Essays," 9–10. Here Nevin agrees with Kant's project, but later he attacks the fundamental premise of the second *Critique* with an argument that sounds fundamentally like Schiller's (*On the Aesthetic Education of Man*), but without mention of Schiller: "Nor will it be possible for the law, in the same circumstances, to acknowledge or respect the independence of the human subject. It must necessarily assume the tone of command, arraying against him the majesty of its own everlasting nature, and with the weight of its terrible categoric imperative[sic], *Thou Shalt*, crushing his liberty completely to the earth" (*Human Freedom*, 14). Nevin's essays demonstrate a growing interest in the method of Hegel, Schleiermacher, and the mediating school, especially in his frequent use of the metaphor "organic unity."

8. This is by no means an exhaustive list, nor can the influence of the romanticists, or of Lessing and Schiller, among others, be disregarded. However, the above list represents the names most often on the lips of the next generation of philosophers and certainly of Mercersburg.

Hegel's Critique of Kant

Georg Wilhelm Friedrich Hegel (1770–1831) was clearly the most important philosopher for Mercersburg. Hegel's philosophical work, especially as developed and modified by the later German mediating school, provided Mercersburg an intellectual foundation and historical perspective, thereby establishing the idealist approach within which Mercersburg engaged American realism. Like so many philosophers of his age, Hegel was equally adept in the fields of history and theology.

Friedrich Ernst Daniel Schleiermacher (1768–1834), a leading theologian of his day, must be ranked with Hegel as making foundational contributions to Mercersburg's concept of philosophy, theology, and history. Like Hegel, Schleiermacher could navigate the philosophical and historical currents with the same confidence that he charted unexplored regions of theology. While bitter rivals, the two held remarkably similar views about the nature of "knowing."[9]

Friedrich Wilhelm Joseph von Schelling (1775–1854) requires mention as well. In many respects Schelling led the way in departing from Kant and Fichte, with Hegel following suit. Schelling's most important influence on Mercersburg came in his "second," later stage of philosophical development.[10]

These philosophers and theologians inspired German idealism and gave it its unique speculative methodology even in the adjustments made by their students, both of the radical and conservative schools that followed (most notably, for Mercersburg, the more conservative, German mediating school). And while no member of the Mercersburg triad can be labeled with one of these philosophers' names, as the leading German scholars of their day, they made huge contributions to the Mercersburg theology, especially as they led Mercersburg away from Kant and toward the speculative theology that would define them.

As young philosophers, Schelling and Hegel believed they had uncovered in Kant an impediment that impoverished the human quest

---

9. For a keen analysis of what they shared and where they differed see Crouter, "Hegel and Schleiermacher at Berlin: A Many Sided Debate."

10. Schelling's philosophic sojourn took him from romantic enthusiast to favored status as apologist for liberal, Roman Catholic theologians. After sharing a close correspondence, they parted company over Hegel's published phenomenology. In 1841 Schelling was called to Berlin to combat the influence of Hegel's disciples, during what is also called Schelling's "theistic period."

for knowledge.[11] It was a criticism that Mercersburg would share and that would convince them that Hegel had made a necessary correction to Kant, although their agreement with Hegel was never systematically articulated, but rather appeared in their wholehearted agreement that Hegel had moved beyond Kant.

Schelling and Hegel found disconcerting Kant's worrisome care not to say too much about what could not be established by sense experience, which they believed led to a contrived and untenable dualism. With a few other critical philosophers, Schelling and Hegel felt that Kant's science of "things seen" denigrated the transcendental experience of "things unseen." But Schelling and Hegel led the way, and they were adamant in their protest that Kant posited a two-tiered universe of worlds composed of the knowable "objects of perception" and the entirely unknowable "things in themselves." Ostensibly Kant had declared metaphysical claims off limits to scientific investigation: religion had its boundaries. Yet here, insisted Schelling and Hegel, was an entire realm, a realm beyond the senses; the realm of "the thing in itself," that was said to exist, without the possibility of having an objective and truly reliable experience of it.[12]

Today undergraduate students know Kant by the epithet "agnostic," even though he was a "believer." What Kant meant to say was that a science of natural phenomena is inappropriate for verifying religious claims. In this he felt he was vindicating Christianity's appeal to faith. Briefly put, Kant was asking, what would be the point of faith if the claims of religion were verifiable? The objection of Schelling and Hegel was that in order to save faith from reason, Kant had to leave the world illegitimately dichotomized and ultimately unknowable. It was one thing to limit knowledge, but quite another to deduce from ignorance the existence of limited being: the result of sustaining a concept of "the thing in itself."[13]

11. In their early years at the university in Jena, Schelling and Hegel edited *The Critical Journal of Philosophy* (1802–3).

12. "If consciousness knows itself in its ultimate nature—and such is Hegel's contention—one half of reality is taken out of the obscurity in which, on Kant's reading of the situation, it is condemned to lie hidden. Man is more knowable than nature, and is the key to nature; such is Hegel's position crudely stated." See Smith, *Commentary On Kant's "Critique of Pure Reason,"* xlv.

13. Kant's "materialistic tendency" retained a concept of "things-in-themselves" (*noumena*), which, Hegel claimed, could not be said to depend on the categories of

Kant believed science could not disprove religion. The dualism of the seen world and the unseen world remained in force. But in order to salvage the unseen world from the perspective of the seen world, a bridge needed to be built. From the time of Descartes, the bridge was "mind." It remained mind for Kant, though he often called it "being." But when Kant gave mind a creative role, the result was a self-intuiting object with independent, ontological status. Hegel maintained that Kant had created what he said was impossible. He had violated his own injunction against perceiving a "transcendental object"[14] by proceeding as if the transcendent mind had objective status (something that Kant argued could only be said for the objects of experience).

Not that Kant claimed the mind could be the object of experience, in the ordinary sense of seeing or perceiving an object. But, reasoned Hegel, his arguments had the same effect. Likewise, Hegel couldn't take Kant's agnosticism seriously. For Hegel, Kant's arguments led to a "mind" that had objective status while never being an object of perception, which was a logical outcome of a philosophy based on sensual intuition.[15]

---

logic developed by Kant. This was so because the logic was applied subjectively to the objects of experience. Yet if this were the case, said Hegel, and we have no grounds for knowing anything beyond experience, neither have we any grounds for maintaining that the categories are purely subjective, for that too would require an intuition that Kant claims we cannot have. Hegel would treat "thingness" (the *noumena*) as a category itself. For more on this, see his *Phenomenology of Mind*, Section II, "Perception: or Things and Their Deceptiveness."

14. "All representations have, as representations, their object, and can themselves in turn become objects of other representations. Appearances are the sole objects which can be given to us immediately, and that in them which relates immediately to the object is called intuition. But these appearances are not the things in themselves; they are only representations, which in turn have their object—an object which cannot itself be intuited by us, and which may, therefore, be named the non-empirical, that is, transcendental object = x" (Kant, *Critique of Pure Reason*, 137).

15. Kant examined consciousness "critically" by assigning logical categories in order to distinguish the aspects of consciousness. He distinguished between passivity and activity (in terms of receiving and acting on sense data), between matter and form, between concept and sensation. But, says Hegel, how are the categories themselves known? All of the distinctions depend on categories imposed by a "reason" without experience. They require a pure intuition. "Instead of the inner activity and self-movement of its own actual life, such a simple determination of direct intuition (*Anschauung*)—which means here sense knowledge—is predicated in accordance with a superficial analogy, and this external and empty application of the formula is called 'construction.'" See Hegel, *Phenomenology of Mind*, 108.

Hegel's conclusion was that knowing is an intuitive process of the mind. Being and knowing are unified in a self-substantiating experience. Individual consciousness recognizes an immediate unity with the objects of perception and the one who perceives, along with the identification of those objects of perception with our ideas of them. But, at the same time, consciousness recognizes that the thoughts are not the objects of perception, but our ideas of them. In short, Hegel identified the process of knowing as a rational phenomenon of nature, and he argued that in the dialectical process of knowing, the objects of perception are at once identical and distinct from the mental images we have of them. The process of knowing is a natural, noetic evolution of the species into higher levels of thought.

The crucial break from all that had gone before signaled the end of classical dualism. Hegel's approach anticipated a time when no longer would there be separate worlds of mind and body, no longer twin but opposed peaks of reality from which came different orders of "facts," one spiritual (or ethical), one empirical. Hegel's philosophy proposed that all of life be seen as unified in a single reality. The individual parts of life distinguished themselves in experience, and were once again found indistinguishable in the "whole," like separate pieces of one great puzzle. And the grand metaphor supporting a system in which "every speck of dust is an organization" was *organic union*.[16]

Romanticism and the Identity Philosophy

The metaphor "organic union" was borrowed directly from the German romantics, and to some extent Hegel and Schleiermacher are products of romantic influence; thus Mercersburg would inherit some romantic impulses.[17] Indeed, Schleiermacher began as a romantic, and German romanticism was a fundamental source in the next generation's attack on Kant and the development of phenomenology and the identity philoso-

---

16. R. C. Solomon recognized the predominance of this concept in the philosophical writing of the period observing that for such influential writers as Holderlin "Nature and Spirit" was the "Grand Metaphor." ". . . the German Ideal typically stressed 'man's unity with nature,' a unity that seemed to have been lost in the complexities of modern society" (*In the Spirit of Hegel*, 58.) The metaphor of "organic unity with nature" is evident in both German idealistic and romantic literature. It was ultimately connected with Hegel's concept of *Geist*, as a unifying principle that gave identity to all existence.

17. As argued by Nichols in his *Romanticism in American Theology*.

phy of Schelling and Hegel. The "unity of being" and the importance of experience were central themes, as was the organic connectedness of all life. Romanticism's emphasis on human experience had a Promethean element, whose residue is evident in the later developments within German idealism. Some romantics believed that virtually any limit to human experience could be overcome. But, with the publication of Schleiermacher's famous *Religion: Speeches to its Cultured Despisers* in 1893, he had broken with Schlegel[18] and departed from the romantic agenda. No longer was he concerned with "perceiving a reality beyond this world." Instead, with other idealists of his age, he sought an experience of the "infinite in the finite;" he sought God among men and women; he sought the reconciliation of faith and reason.[19]

The limits to be overcome had long been established by a predominant German philosophical temperament called "rationalism." Romanticism reacted negatively to rationalism's "cold" detachment from experience. The new German idealists inherited much of that negative reaction. The criticism on the part of idealists was that rationalism had obviated the chief aim of religion, which was to establish "real" and meaningful contact or relationship with the Almighty (or the transcendent). Contact and relationship with God was being denied by rationalism's removal of God from the world of experience. Schleiermacher and Hegel, along with most German idealists, believed that the duty of religion was to recover the divine for human experience. Philosophy's role was to provide opportunity for experience, and not, as rationalism would have it, to prescribe its precinct.[20]

"Supernaturalistic rationalists" was the epithet used by both Hegel and Schleiermacher to describe the general mind-set of the earlier and,

---

18. Friedrich Schlegel (1772–1829) was a leading romantic author who borrowed heavily from Greek ideals.

19. Forstman, *Romantic Triangle: Schleiermacher and Early German Romanticism*, 115–19.

20. Certainly the way this was done differed among the thinkers, yet the goal was the same, "The all-important question—and we are back where we began—is whether human reason can know God" (Lauer, *Hegel's Concept of God*, 287–89), and "There can be no question that the modern spirit of philosophical inquiry, the beginning of which Hegel finds in Descartes, has effected a separation of the human thinking subject from that which had previously been conceived of as ruling that spirit from above" (Lauer, *Hegel's Concept of God*, 16).

in their minds, now discredited thinkers of their age.[21] The speculative philosophers and theologians criticized the rationalists for paying quasi-spiritual lip service to "faith in God" and the "biblical witness" while lampooning any attempt at scientific support for such a faith. They felt cheated by systems that plead ignorance in concluding that God exists "transcendentally."

A new weapon in the idealist's philosophical arsenal was the unique development of their age. It was referred to as "speculative science." Originally, Schelling and Hegel termed it the "identity philosophy."[22] Soon it would come to dominate philosophy in Prussia and provide the epistemological foundation for the humanistic sciences' incredible breakthroughs in history, comparative religion, and sociology. Speculative philosophy operated on the premise of a phenomenology of intrinsic spiritual unity (*Geist*). All of life could be described dialectically, in terms of a polarity between the finite and the infinite.

Hegel outlined the process for thinking beings: Life unfolds itself in our experience of other beings, objects, ideas—all of which become known by virtue of the limits we place on them. We know the world by separating out experience. Yet as the very process of life, the limits we set on things in order to "know" them—these limits must share in the identity of the things known. Still, no matter how much we limit our experience, we must recognize that every object of experience, each life, each idea, even the inanimate object, resists these limits, indeed, defies them.

Hegel believed that our thoughts about things change constantly, and in that, so evolves the "identity" of the object. God comes to us as

---

21. Mercersburg would adopt the term picking it up from the German mediating school's critique of rationalism.

22. Schelling developed the *Identitätphilosophie* over several publications, beginning with *Bruno, Oder über das göttliche und natürliche Prinzip der Dinge* (1802). Early on, Hegel defended it, but later he coined the term "speculative philosophy" for what was a similar methodology. Hegel's unique understanding of the "Absolute" constituted the significant departure from Schelling. Yet in their initial criticism of Kant and Fichte, they forged a philosophy of identity, with Schelling leading the way. "In philosophical knowledge, what is united is an activity of both intelligence and nature, of consciousness and the unconscious together. It belongs to both worlds at once, the ideal and the real. It belongs to the ideal world because it is posited in intelligence and, hence, in freedom. It belongs to the real world because it gets its place in the objective totality; it is deduced as a link in the chain of necessity." See Hegel, *Difference between Fichte's and Schelling's System of Philosophy*, 110.

the supreme example of this principle, having unlimited, infinite being, which never changes, yet, which, by limiting itself, becomes known through a series of revelations, the "absolute" of which, for Hegel, is the manifestation of Jesus Christ in the Trinity: the many unified in the One.[23]

Schleiermacher operated from a somewhat different framework. Both thinkers share an encompassing, systematic approach that would explain the "way it is," that is, the way the infinite is present in the finite, or, quite simply, the way we know God. But for Schleiermacher, the beginning of the process of discovering God, in fact, its operative principle, is fundamentally emotion, or emotion's determinative force: will. This contrasts with Hegel's more traditional emphasis on reason.[24]

In Schleiermacher the romantic influence is deeply evident. Consciousness asserts itself as a self-determining "will" that "feels" itself as such. This feeling recognizes its utter dependence on another as the ground of its existence (its "being"). The "freedom to know" contains the requirement to acknowledge that one is not the source of all that is.

Hegel would never allow emotion to rule experience, even though the contribution of romantic thought to his own thinking cannot be overlooked. But a noncognitive approach was unsatisfactory to him. He feared such an approach threatened the objectivity of God, as well as God's autonomy.

In spite of their differences, idealists posed a challenge to classical dualism that was formidable. The philosophical result was a paradigmatic

---

23. "Die Theologie drückt in der Weise der Vorstellung diesen Prozeß bekanntlick so aus, daß Gott der Vater (dies einfach Allgemeine, Insichseiende), seine Einsamkeit aufgebend, die Natrue (das Sichselbstäußerliche, Außeersichseiende) erschafft, einen Sohn (sein anderes ich) erzeugt, in diesem Anderen aber kraft seiner unendlichen Liebe sich selbst anschaut, darin sein Ebenbild erkennt und in demselben zur Einheit mit sich zurückkehrt; welche nicht mehr abstrakte, unmittelbare, sondern konkrete, durch den Unterschied vermittelte Einheit der vom Vater und vom Sohne ausgehende, in der christlichen Gemeine zu siener vollkommenen Wirklichkeit und Wahrheit gelangende heilige Geist ist, als welcher Gott erkannt werden muß, wenn er in siner absoluten Wahrheit." See Hegel, Werke 10, *Enzyklopädie der philosophischen Wissenschaften im Grundrisse* (1830; rpt. Frankfurt: Suhrkamp, 1970) 23.

24. "Under the influence of Kant and Fichte the 'theologians' of Hegel's day—with Jacobi and Schleiermacher in the vanguard—were opting for an intuitive grasp, an emotional response, a worship of they knew not what; but Hegel would have none of this. He preferred the attitude of the medieval Scholastics, whose philosophy was continuous with their theology" (Lauer, *Hegel's Concept of God*," 288–89).

shift away from emphasis on the acceptable limits of experience. Hegel and those who followed him were unified in begrudging the world a dual identity. For them, such pandering to the Cartesian view of the world as partly seen, partly unseen, hence partly known, partly unknown, produced the irresistible temptation toward the extremes of skepticism and mysticism. Instead, they insisted that the so-called unseen world was really the horizon of the one and only seen world. They believed that God was intentional about not hiding anything. Indeed, God was actively involved in the process of revelation. Nor did God create two ontologically opposed universes. Rather, God created one world, whose nature it was to realize itself in successive stages of development.

In place of the several unwelcome alternatives being considered by philosophers of the early eighteenth century, the speculative approach offered a unified, developmental model of a world disclosing itself in historical stages, each stage growing out of the other. The organic connectedness of things revealed that knowing is also growing. True knowledge is not so much the accumulation of facts but recognizing and organizing these facts into a complete and comprehensive picture. Being right or wrong isn't simply a matter of the reliability of the senses, or the accuracy of one's impressions. Being "right" meant being sensitive to the process (the phenomenon) and the conclusions (the new stage) that the facts might point to. Being wrong usually meant failing to find one's moment in the Absolute,[25] to wit, the cardinal sin of recalcitrant philosophers: not recognizing how one's experience is being shaped and ultimately "negated" by the relentless tide of history.

The German Mediating School

In the years that followed Hegel's success, his philosophy was split into schools of the "left" and "right." The left held firmly to the unity of experience, which ultimately led them in the direction of materialism.[26] The

---

25. Hegel's famous criticism (aimed at Schelling) spoke of "the night in which all cows are black," the absurd result when everything is nothing and nothing is everything. In this case, Hegel would likely point to the emptiness of Schelling's Absolute as evidence that his was an eclipsed philosophy.

26. The history of materialism is as ancient as that of idealism, and throughout the years changes have occurred in the schools, but, briefly stated, materialism tends to understand reality as constituted in matter as the physical manifestation of all that is. Hegel's student, Karl Marx, is likely the most well-known example of that era's materialism.

right retained a subtle or understated dualism.[27] In part, this reflected Schleiermacher's strong disagreement with Hegel. Schleiermacher sustained the mystery of life. For him, there was a part of life beyond human reason and, so, forever unknown. He could not condone Hegel's concept of "absolute knowledge."[28] Hegel's system, on the other hand, depended on the unity of knowledge and experience. But more in keeping with their conservative role, these students of the "right" pined for orthodoxy, they sought solidarity with Christian tradition, and so they embraced a confessional language rife with talk of the "two worlds."

Predictably, the conservatives rejoiced that Hegel and Schleiermacher had recovered God for human experience, but they rejected the possibility that speculative philosophy might obviate the divine mystery.[29] They felt something of the spiritual realm remained invisible and beyond their grasp. Furthermore, they valued orthodoxy above philosophical consistency. While this clearly weakened their argument, they simply embraced the bulk of Hegel's system, while passionately holding to a concept that held back a portion of heaven from human experience (something Hegel himself would not tolerate). They seemed unaware of (or at least unwilling to address) the latent dualism that hung like the proverbial "skeleton" in their (philosophical) closet.

As for the extreme left wing, frustration with bourgeoisie political institutions led some of Hegel's students (e.g., Karl Marx) to view his philosophy as an ideology bolstering the status quo, and thus, itself, "a moment to be negated."[30] On the other hand, many conservatives, fearing the revolution in France, sought simply to "soften" Hegel in order

---

27. The right in large part represents the philosophers, theologians, and historians of the mediating school.

28. Schleiermacher wrote, "All real philosophy consists in the insight that this inexpressible truth of the highest essence lies at the basis of all our thinking experience, and the development of this insight is itself that very thing which, according to my conviction, Plato construed as dialectic. I don't believe we can get further than this." Quoted by Crouter, "Hegel and Schleiermacher," 24.

29. In Philip Schaff's controversial *Principle of Protestantism*, he articulated the fears of the earlier mediating school, writing that in Kant's grafting a moral system to an intense spirit of practical piety, he paved the way to the unlicensed, speculative "desolation" of the Hegelian "left," a type of rationalism that is "god unto itself, pretending it has no need of a moral defense" (100).

30. This is precisely the premise of Marx's "The Holy Family." See also Marx's *Critique of Hegel's "Philosophy of Right."*

to continue enjoying the support of the monarchy. Still other conservatives were being attracted to a movement called neopietism.[31]

Neopietism called for a return to traditional Protestant values and conservative faith. It emphasized a faith founded on the confessions and on a "personal experience of salvation in Jesus Christ." Its appeal was enormous, spreading throughout Germany, and eventually replacing Hegelian influence at Prussian universities (1845). Schaff himself was intimately associated with neopietism. He claimed a "conversion experience" at an early age, and his formative training and education were at the hands of many pietist leaders.[32] Yet, neopietism seemed excessive to him. Too much of reason was given up for "feeling." Other, somewhat older, conservative students of Schleiermacher and Hegel felt the same. They were convinced that neopietism's overemphasis of personal experience to the detriment of all else led to the decentralizing of confessional orthodoxy and the ultimate loss of Protestant unity and identity.[33]

In response, many of the new generation of theologians, historians, and church leaders, influenced by idealism, initiated a program that would mediate between traditionalism and German speculative theology. The loose confederation of these like-minded thinkers became known as the mediating school of theology. Philosophically and theologically, the mediating school was the most important direct influence on Mercersburg. Yet in terms of ecclesiology, liturgy, and the place of the sacraments, the High-Church wing of the neopietist party held sway for the Mercersburg school.[34]

---

31. Marilyn Massey calls neopietism "dogmatic ecclesiasticism." She defines it as "a hybrid of orthodoxy and Pietism." It was formed "when a revival of the emphasis of adherence to traditional Lutheran dogmas as the mark of authentic Christian faith was coupled with the Pietist stress on the inner relationship of the believer to Christ, a relationship found in the heart, not the mind." See Massey, *Christ Unmasked*, 44.

32. Philip Schaff's formative education was in Korntal, Württemberg, and Stuttgart, each a Pietist stronghold. After a period in Tübigen, Schaff went to the university in Halle where he came under the influence of the neopietist theologian, Tholuck. Tholuck introduced Schaff to many of the movement's leaders. From there Schaff went to Berlin and met the neopietist E. W. Hengstenberg. James Hastings Nichols wrote that at that time, Hengstenberg was "the most powerful ecclesiastical politician in Prussia" (*Mercersburg Theology*, 6). Finally Leopold and Ludwig von Gerlach added a churchly element to Schaff's exposure to neopietism.

33. See Philip Schaff, *Person of Christ*, 7–8.

34. Little has been written on Nevin's interest in mediating thought; however, he included his own translation of an essay by Karl Ullmann called "The Distinctive

Nevin joined Schaff in both praising and condemning Schleiermacher, and in identifying the mediating school as the significant purveyors of contemporary Christian theological science. Said Nevin, Schleiermacher must be commended for addressing the spread of rationalism in Germany. He stopped infidelity in its tracks and restored faith to his generation of Christians, and he did it intelligently and convincingly. Yet his was an incomplete system, still overly influenced by German rationalism and, so, weak in its doctrine of sin. Fortunately, concluded Nevin and Schaff, his students improved on the work of their teacher.[35]

These "students" (not all having studied with Schleiermacher, but under his influence) were the mediating school of philosophers, historians, theologians, and pastors. They were among the most significant and influential thinkers of their age: men like Dorner, Rothe, Ullmann, Nitzsch, Daub, and Neander. They were the so-called liberals of their generation. (Although they were more theologically orthodox than Schleiermacher and Hegel, they distanced themselves from the age's true conservatives, the pietists). Yet they were marked by the imprint of their teachers. After all, they were still heavily influenced by Schleiermacher, and they universally adopted the speculative approach. Yet what distinguished them from other idealists, especially those who had gone before, was their view of Scripture—as reliable and authoritative. Where they remained idealists was in their understanding of life as "organic," and in their understanding of history as a dialectical and upward progression. Where they wavered and diverged was in the way they understood the unity of experience, their strict acceptance of

---

Character of Christianity" as a manifesto and preface to his *Mystical Presence*. It was originally published in *Theologische Studien und Kritiken* in 1845. Ullmann was a leading mediating theologian. In addition, Rauch undoubtedly, but without clear evidence, influenced Nevin in the direction of mediating thought. When Rauch left Germany, he was of the mediating mind-set. For a deeper analysis of this see my article, "Frederick Augustus Rauch: First American Hegelian," 70–77. On the other hand, Schaff's involvement with the mediating school is well documented. Some of the finest work on this has been done by Klaus Penzel in, for example, "Reformation Goes West," 219–41. Also significant are the works of George Schriver: "Philip Schaff: America's Destiny in the Unfinished Reformation," 148–59; "Philip Schaff as a Teacher of Church History," and, "Philip Schaff's Concept of Organic Historiography," Other works include Johnson, "Mustard Seed and the Leaven," 117–70; and Trost, "Philip Schaff's Concept of the Church."

35. Nevin, *Antichrist: Or the Spirit of Sect and Schism*, 100.

ancient Christian orthodoxy, and their divergent views of the authority of the church.

History and the New Philosophy

While the principle philosophic river that fed the Mercersburg system was speculative theology, there were many tributaries providing precious richness to Mercersburg's flow of ideas. Mercersburg relied on the mediating school's reworking of German idealism and the speculative approach to orient them in the mainstream of contemporary Protestant thinking, where the Reformation doctrine of the faithfulness and reliability of Scripture was still revered. From neopietism they borrowed the confessional motif that provided a Protestant, confessional unity against the latitudinarians among the mediating school. The Oxford movement was not without appreciation as a serious, if flawed, model of catholicity.[36] Yet the selective borrowing and adapting of philosophic (and to a lesser extent, theological) ideas were done to address the very same issue originally addressed by Schelling, Schleiermacher, and Hegel: the breach of faith and reason.

It was the philosophical problem of rationalism and the removal of God from the human arena that provoked Mercersburg's reactionary efforts. If there was a big picture, it was their comprehensive and well-orchestrated response to infidelity on the one hand, and their over-

---

36. The Oxford movement (1833–1845) in England sought to restore the high-church ideals of the 1600s. Under the leadership of such capable men as Newman, Pusey, and Wilberforce, its wide distribution of essays, pamphlets, and articles led many to refer to it as the Tractarian movement. These tracts influenced Nevin and Schaff, and Schaff visited Pusey in England. Most importantly they shared the ideal of the necessary unity of the one Catholic and Apostolic Church, but this shared ideal was also the source of their fundamental disagreement. The Oxonians' notion of apostolic succession within the Anglican Church astonished Mercersburg. Both Schaff and Nevin were convinced that it was an inauthentic stand. Furthermore, Schaff never regarded physical succession as necessary; rather he argued for a spiritual succession, as in the case of St. Paul. Yet perhaps the most telling criticism is also the most revealing of the true source of Mercersburg's inspiration: "It is only ridiculous however to fancy the English Church, or the Episcopal Church in America, on any sort of parallel and level, as regards theological science, with German Protestantism under its better form" (Nevin, "Wilberforce on the Incarnation," 164). Still, Nevin concedes the point that when it comes to their use of the creeds as the foundation for sound Christian practice and belief, "our theology is more Anglican than German." See Nevin, "Our Relations to Germany," 632.

zealous or blind adherence to a passion-born faith—as in American revivalism—on the other. German idealism and the speculative theology provided the grand scheme of history.[37] It was this "superior," almost Promethean advantage over history that gave the idealist historians such confidence when unearthing the cause of what was commonly believed to be the century's malaise and resulting disquiet.

The history and interpretation of the ancient biblical texts occupied the oldest member of the Mercersburg triad. Born in 1803, John W. Nevin briefly taught Hebrew at Princeton, where he obtained his degree, and took over Hodge's course while the latter traveled in Germany. The study of Hebrew and the history of the biblical texts and stories was a field dominated by the Germans who had pioneered the science of hermeneutics, and these scholars typically hailed from the rationalist school. Nevin's interests would soon broaden, but his first encounter with German science was with the rationalists' methods imported from Germany by Andover. He later confessed nearly being "seduced by their temperament."[38]

Coincidentally, the youngest of the Mercersburg trio, Philip Schaff (born in 1819), eventually made the study of church history his career. Nevin and Schaff shared an early appreciation of August Neander, the German mediating school's premier historian, and they adhered to Hegel's concept of the dialectical progression of history through successive stages.[39]

History's determinative progress was a cardinal tenet of the Hegelians, and Frederick Rauch, born between Nevin and Schaff (in 1806), but first to arrive at Mercersburg, boldly established the foundation of the seminary in the modern Hegelian mode.[40] Rauch began his professional life as a philologist in Germany, but immigrated to America

---

37. Richard Rorty has written, in "Life at the End of Inquiry," that Hegel's legacy was "a series of philosophical movements which tried to historicize epistemology, seeing in history the same sort of sovereign arbiter that earlier philosophers found in God or Nature," (review of *Realism and Reason*, 6).

38. Nevin, *My Own Life*, 143.

39. As persuaded by the mediating thought, they adopted the modified view developed by Neander.

40. Indeed Rauch's campaign to establish an all German curriculum at the seminary alienated his American colleague Lewis Mayer who was a practitioner of common-sense realism. The conflict is recorded in Good, *History of the Reformed Church in the U.S. in the Nineteenth Century*, 106.

when it became obvious that a career in Germany was unlikely.[41] Rauch knew and admired the great mediating philosopher Carl Daub, to whom Hegel had entrusted the correcting and revising of the second edition of his *Enzyclopädie* (1827). Rauch met with Daub in Heidelberg and undoubtedly discussed with him his views on philosophy. It is likely that Daub tutored Rauch in the subtleties of the Hegelian system.[42]

Rauch's familiarity with the teaching of Hegel and his commitment to Hegel's speculative approach was demonstrated in his *Psychology; Or, A View of the Human Soul Including Anthropology* (1840). Nevin wrote the introduction to the second edition. The work left Nevin with the impression that Rauch was a leading German scholar, and he believed that the *Psychology* was the first American work of the mediating school; original in that it was not merely a reproduction of Hegel's philosophy, but a bold and essentially successful attempt to unite German and American philosophical thought.[43]

This satisfies Rauch's own stated purpose, which was to integrate German idealism with the Scottish informed realism current in America. However, in spite of his Herculean efforts, Rauch simply had not the time to fully comprehend the American philosophy. Truly Rauch seasoned the work with references to the empirical school, but ultimately he failed to synthesize the material as promised. Rather, the *Psychology* employs idealism's methods for understanding human experience. A close reading of his work reveals that in most respects the *Psychology* simply re-creates the third part of Hegel's system.[44] The real genius of the work is its relative clarity. In a remarkably short period of

41. For the full story of Rauch's unhappy departure from Germany, see my review of Rauch's *Psychology; or, a View of the Human Soul*, 87–88.

42. See my "Frederick Rauch," 71–72.

43. Rauch makes his claim of uniting the two systems in his preface (v). Nevin confirms the view in his review of Rauch's *Psychology*.

44. This was put forward by Howard J. B. Ziegler in *Frederick Augustus Rauch, American Hegelian*. That Rauch was neither a disciple of Hegel nor the first American Hegelian was argued by Lloyd Easton in *Hegel's First American Followers*, 9. Although Rauch was the first in America to incorporate Hegel's system into his writing, he differed from Hegel, especially, as Easton points out, in his Protestant orthodoxy. Easton is correct if being a Hegelian requires full conformity to Hegel's philosophy. Oddly, those who knew Rauch personally did not think he was a Hegelian. However, those familiar with his work believed he was. That Rauch was the first American to write from the Hegelian perspective is without question. It may just be that Nevin was closest to the truth when he suggested that Rauch was of the mediating school.

time, Rauch produced a phenomenological vocabulary in English able to reflect Hegel's convoluted system and technical language.

Rauch was engaged by the German Reformed Church to head its seminary in Mercersburg.[45] Correspondence between evangelicals in America and Germany was frequent. The German Reformed church felt itself connected to the homeland, and events occurring in Germany were of great interest. They were desperate for pastors, and appeals for pastoral leaders abounded. The perception of many in Germany was that the immigrants were a type of missionary. Rauch may have felt that sense of mission, leaving the sophistication of Continental academic life to oversee the education of farmers in America. He lost no time transforming the seminary into a center of German study and culture, complete with a Goethe Society.

Perhaps to ease the sense of being out of the mainstream of German intellectual science, Rauch threw himself into his work and study with a vengeance. This led to his exhaustion and may have contributed to his premature death in 1841 at the age of thirty-five. That brought Nevin to the forefront. Nevin inherited Rauch's course on ethics, but more importantly he inherited his lecture notes, which he carefully followed to the conclusion of the course.[46] Perhaps this was out of sense of responsibility to the one whose course it was. More likely, Nevin had replaced the common-sense ethical base of Locke and Edwards with his newfound speculative theology.

Nevin's Puritan upbringing literally reflected the forces of change, which adapted Westminster and the scholastic Calvinism of the seventeenth century. His earliest descriptions of his childhood suggest that he was taught according to the New Light perspective typified by Edwards. By then the Old Lights had faded, and with them the characteristic names that divided them. Orthodoxy evolved only to be challenged by another "new movement" brought by the "second awakening." This time the establishment was branded Old School, while those who yearned for revival, sought the relaxation of denominational ties, and preferred "the plain word of God" over creeds and confessions, came to be called the New School. At Princeton, Nevin sided with the Old School.

---

45. In 1837 the preparatory school became Marshall College and was joined by the seminary of the German Reformed Church, which had moved from Carlisle to Mercersburg.

46. Apple, *Life and Work of John Williamson Nevin*, 422.

This made Nevin a modern, American Calvinist battling on two fronts. In Europe, the threat was rationalism and infidelity. At home, it was growing pluralism, which thrived in the progress and confidence gained by science, and the popularity of an American form of Arminianism, where religion was guided by individual moral conscience. Nevin himself was in turmoil over Old School Calvinism's vulnerability.[47]

The inward sense that provided moral direction implied a faculty able to choose. Edwards believed that God graciously convicted that faculty of both its fallenness and its redemption. Nevin recognized the contradiction. In an early sermon, he was visibly at odds with his theology and upbringing. He mysteriously concluded that the doctrines of free will and predestination are both correct; both grant a perspective of ultimate reality, and he offered the solution in a concept we now call complementarity.[48] The sermon is remarkable for its being out of keeping with the vehement side-taking characteristics of the Old and New School debates.[49]

Neither Rauch nor Schaff knew the history of America's intellectual development. How could they? History itself was a burgeoning science. In America, history was typically the rhetorical narrative of Judeo-Christianity's various dispensations, naturally culminating in the American experience. Schaff would later pioneer the field of historical science, and the slow and wearied appreciation by Schaff for America's religious peculiarities is a study in itself.[50]

Called by the Evangelical and Reformed Church (or the German Reformed Church) to assist Nevin in his duties at the Seminary, Schaff

---

47. Long after Nevin became an idealist, he referred to Old School Calvinism as "metaphysical Calvinism" in Nevin, *My Own Life*.

48. Complementarity is the theory that two seemingly contradictory theories can be correct insofar as they provide insights into actual experience. Niels Bohr first recognized in physics that "A complete elucidation of one and the same object may require diverse points of view which defy a unique description." Ian G. Barbour develops this into the "complementarity principle" in *Myths, Models and Paradigms*, benefiting from the research of C. A. Coulson and D. M. MacKay. For the quote from Bohr, see Barbour, *Myths*, 75.

49. Nevin, "Election Not Contrary to a Free Gospel," 211.

50. Klaus Penzel has written brilliantly on many aspects of Schaff's early development, including his changing view of the American church system. See the texts previously cited.

had no reason to appreciate the subtleties of the Old and New School antagonism. Still, idealism had made a budding historian of Schaff, and eventually he understood perfectly well what the stakes were for America. His solution was simple. Schaff would take the debate to the next level of historical development and incorporate the best learning from the orthodox idealism flourishing in Germany.

Schaff had studied Hegel under F. C. Baur, but he was never convinced by Hegel's "left." Schaff was deeply evangelical. He was also very churchly. His scholarly bent allowed him to remain faithful—as long as he need not repent of reason. Neopietism and the High-Church movement allowed him the luxury of intelligent faith. Hengstenburg, a German leader in the return to traditional Protestant values, was of great influence, as were the Von Gerlach brothers. Confession and creed, ideas being downplayed by rationalists, as well as by America's New School members, were dear to Schaff's heart. So were the sacraments: baptism and the Lord's Supper, two more traditions that New Schoolers and rationalists would downplay as sacred mysteries. New School enthusiasm was for revival preaching and the conversion of souls, while rationalism found its most popular support among Unitarians.

Schelling's Historical Philosophy

The most important foundational philosophic moment of Schaff's life came when he attended the lectures of Schelling in 1841.[51] Schelling had reemerged in Prussia as the philosophically conservative alternative to Hegel. Schelling had revised his system in a Platonic direction and produced his own phenomenology. Simply put, it differed from Hegel's in that the idea or ideal remained paramount. Schelling's idealism still identified the idea as it came to be in history's evolution. However, the material world was not the ideal world, as Hegel would have it.

Schelling's system was attractive to evangelical theologians, as well as Roman Catholics, for the alternative it provided to Hegelianism.[52]

---

51. As reported by his son, David, in *Life of Philip Schaff*, 34. See also Penzel, "Reformation Goes West," 227.

52. For an introduction to Schelling among the Roman Catholic theologians in Germany, see O'Meara, *Romantic Idealism and Roman Catholicism: Schelling and the Theologians*. For an excellent treatment of Continental religious philosophy in the wake of the Romantic era (with a chapter dedicated to Schelling) see Bernard M. G. Reardon, *Religion in the Age of Romanticism*.

Dualism was overcome without allowing materialism to share center stage with the "idea." Schelling made the "real" the organic embodiment of the idea, and in his thirty-sixth and thirty-seventh lectures, given at the university in Berlin, he provided what some believed was the solution to the question of historical progress: While transcendence is a natural phenomenon, the evolution of the historical idea is rational, sequential, and governed by the Absolute (God). Each movement and moment in history merely manifests a higher stage of its original character, which exists in the eternal idea. That idea exists in the prescient experience of every individual.

In other words, the church, for example, may develop into ever-higher stages of its own life, but it may never transcend (negate) its original idea, as that idea was established in the life and work of Jesus. History, then, is the science of the evolving idea. As for the church, its history is the stages where Jesus's prescient experience manifests itself.

Schelling's philosophy explained how the church could develop historically, remain the unblemished bride of Christ in its form, and yet manifest serious deficiencies throughout history. It also explained history's drama, as each new stage appeared where the idea would play itself out. The most recent stage for many idealists was set in America.

Schaff would master American religious history. Indeed he came to pioneer in the field, but not before confessed miscalculations. For example, he miscalculated America's commitment to realism. What he found even more shocking was its aversion to idealism. Conversely, idealism had made history come alive for Schaff and Nevin. Until Schleiermacher and more importantly for Mercersburg, until the mediator, Augustus Neander, with dubious but unavoidable mention of the brilliant and yet frightening, later work of Strauss (*The Life of Jesus*), history was flat and dogmatic. Hegel provided the dynamic dialectic of thesis, antithesis, and synthesis, thus placing men and women within the historical currents.[53] Idealists believed that our destinies were no longer outside these currents, but within them, controlled by them; and

---

53. During the 1840s Hegel's students applied his approach to society and politics. Schaff's thinking here is obviously influenced by them. Foremost in working out the dialectical triad of the world's historical development was August von Cieszkowski. For more on this, see the articles by Lawrence S. Stepelevich briefly summarized and cited in Stepelevich, "Eucharistic Theory: Hegelianism and Mercersburg Theology."

the study of these currents provided insight into the future, as well as "real" knowledge of the past.

It could be argued that Schelling's contribution was even more ambitious than Hegel's, certainly with regard to what might be anticipated in the future. Hegel's limit was history's inherent unpredictability. The substance of history must await its appearance in actual history.[54] Schelling argued that Hegel made the idea produce the substance of history. The charge was that Hegel could not explain how pure thought moves to objective nature. The criticism was that although thought can reflect on history's movement, it cannot produce it! In contrast, Schelling believed that human experience contains the facts of history, such that consciousness provides the key to unlocking the mystery of history's progress. As one comes to understand one's culture, its history, science, people, and art, one is able to anticipate history's course.

Unlike Hegel, Schelling made the real subservient to the ideal, thus restricting development to what is prefigured in the past. Civilization's development is proleptic. Transcendence occurs as each stage further develops the original idea.

In some popular thought, this became the salvation of idealism for the orthodox. Left-wing Hegelians, like Baur and Rothe, had been describing the next stage of the church's development, identifying it with the state. This was consistent with a developmental model that had each stage negate and thus transcend its former stage. What the church is becoming and will someday be, may be entirely different from what it started out as.

Schelling's philosophy allowed no such development. Schelling maintained that the original idea cannot transcend itself, and so he provided his readers a glimpse of the future based entirely on the past. For Schelling, Jesus established the church, and he is the organic seed upon

---

54. Hegel wrote in the preface to his *Philosophy of Right* (12–13): "One more word about teaching what the world ought to be: Philosophy always arrives too late to do any such teaching. As the *thought* of the world, philosophy appears only in the period after actuality has been achieved and has completed its formative process. The lesson of the concept, which necessarily is also taught by history, is that only in the ripeness of actuality does the ideal appear over against the real, and that only then does this ideal comprehend this same real world in its substance and build it up for itself into the configuration of an intellectual realm. When philosophy paints its gray in gray, then a configuration of life has grown old, and cannot be rejuvenated by this gray in gray, but only understood; the Owl of Minerva takes flight only as the dusk begins to fall."

which all subsequent development depends. His choice as successor, St. Peter, established the Romanistic and legalistic quality of the evolving church. In Peter the church found structure and strength, if also developing a dogmatic inflexibility. In antithesis, St. Paul established a Protestant-like principle of freedom, and aroused the church's evangelical spirit. But a third and final synthesis remained below the surface, awaiting the full negation of Protestant sectarian madness and Roman entrenchment, and that was the church of St. John, ruled by the principle of love, and governed by Christ's irenic commandment for unity.

The Mediating Foundation

Although Mercersburg was generally more "churchly" than the German mediating philosophers, theologians, and historians, they shared a single undertaking in seeking to balance the influences of pietism and rationalism. Nitzsch, Dorner, Ullmann, Neander, Rothe, and Daub all worked within the idealist tradition, inheriting Kant's program to recover the material principle of divine participation in human history, and to wrest from rationalism its domination of German intellectual life. They believed that the rationalistic thinkers lured Christianity into rejecting its mystical foundations. Such was the effect, they argued, of losing sight of the material principle. The result was widespread defection from the faith. In order to reverse this harmful tendency, the mediators were led to a central unifying dogma: the incarnation.

If alienation from God was the problem, reconciliation and reunion were the solution. Thus the mediators argued that God's participation in human experience was a historical fact commencing with the life, work, death, and resurrection of Jesus. For them, the "Christ event" was the watershed of human history. This brought Christology to the fore, not just of their theology, but of their epistemology as well. Mercersburg made the person of Christ the key to absolute knowledge.[55]

55. Even the philosophical method of Rauch followed Hegel's prescription by making Christianity the ultimate religion. However, Rauch departed from Hegel in arguing that reason cannot achieve absolute knowledge. Faith is required to supply what reason cannot. For a glimpse into Rauch's orthodoxy, see his "Every Man Is the Lord's," 221–31; "Faith and Reason," 80–94; and *Inner Life of the Christian*. As for the other founders of the movement, Schaff's piety placed theology above philosophy, and Nevin's articles on Cyprian (*Mercersburg Review*, 1852) maintained that unless the philosopher began with the confession, as in the Apostles' Creed, his or her knowledge of reality will remain incomplete.

If a philosopher was to make progress in understanding life and reality, the philosopher needed the knowledge of God exclusively available through Christ.

Taking their cue from the mediating school, Mercersburg concluded that the key to unlocking the mystery of philosophical truth and life's meaning eluded rationalists because they proceeded inductively. Christ alone held the key to unlocking the mystery of life, and only christological science could address philosophy's misdirection. Indeed, so lost was this present rationalistic age, that the mediators perceived it as an age of "universal spiritual chaos."[56]

The mediators' historical critique depended on Hegelian science. The argument was that former mystic romanticism was ill equipped to address rationalism and could only brood over rationalism's sanctioning experience according to the limits of reason. While many of the romantics were valiant in their witness that the world inwardly longed for the reconciliation of faith and reason, they had no science that could reverse the evil trend. In deference to Kant, he was credited with the discovery of the absolute autonomy of the human will, thus putting philosophy back on course. Likewise his successor, Fichte, was praised for recognizing that subjective experience must be the absolute measure of reality. Still, Schelling and Hegel concluded that latent skepticism would rebound into extreme objectivity.

Turning against their teachers, many of the mediating school, with Mercersburg in full agreement, suggested that in Hegel and Schelling, the antithetical worlds of faith and reason were united, but not without serious damage to many orthodox doctrines. Most significantly, for the mediators, was the damage done to the Augustinian concept of sin as an ontological force recognized within the human soul and operative in the world.[57]

It was left to the next generation of theologians to mediate between the speculative insights of the philosophers and those who would simply repristinate the past. Again, the solution offered by the mediators was the very person and work of Christ as a recovery of the material

---

56. Nevin makes this case in "Dorner's History of Protestant Theology: Second Article," 352.

57. In book 2.7 of Augustine's *Confessions*, the human race is completely culpable, loving evil simply because it is evil. The development of this aspect of Western theology is usefully explained in Brooks Otis, *Dumbarton Oaks Papers*, vol. 12.

(objective) principle to balance the age's utter preoccupation with the formal (subjective) principle. They concluded that pure subjectivity, as expressed in rationalism's flirt with freedom and in the license given individuals to interpret Scripture without confessional restraint, threatened to strip Protestantism of its integrity. The material principle was required to ground Protestants in objectivity and retrieve the gospel's center, which was a living, divine presence operating in the world through the church.

Mercersburg was convinced that the most important philosophical issue facing the age was the breach of faith and reason, with no thanks to rationalism, whose skeptical bent forced limits, indeed, impoverished the most sublime and meaningful experiences of life, all according to the newest shibboleth: empirical science (more often called rationalism).[58] For many, Gilead's balm was found in common-sense philosophy. That was the case with many scholars in England and America (along with a few in Germany). However, the leaders of the mediating school were far from satisfied. For them, practical realism simply supported the antagonism by holding the worlds of sense and spirit apart. As far as Mercersburg was concerned, philosophically sophisticated theological science had progressed beyond the classical debate of realism and nominalism. Nineteenth-century psychology's revolutionary discovery was the unity of experience in consciousness, where all that would be fact and fiction could and must be measured according to speculative science. Many in Europe and the Continent believed that the theologians most adept at bringing recent scientific discoveries to bear on the problem of faith were the mediating scholars, where, according to Mercersburg, theological science had reached its apex in the "Christological struggles" of the period.[59]

---

58. This is especially the case with Nevin, whose warnings about trusting too much in science and technology took on a prophetic tone. See his "Commencement Address" to the class at Franklin and Marshall College, Lancaster, Pennsylvania, 25 July 1867. In contrast, the most important theological issue of the age for Mercersburg was the "Church Question" i.e., the eclipse of the Protestant Church's catholicity.

59. The term "Christological struggles" is taken directly from Carl Ullmann in his "Distinctive Character of Christianity."

3

Mercersburg and Princeton

MERCERSBURG WAS WELL AWARE OF THE SIGNIFICANCE OF PRINCETON'S rejection of German speculative theology. They knew that the various controversies sparked by their movement would be judged (in the minds of many evangelical Americans) according to the Princeton tribunal, and it came as a blow to Nevin and Schaff that Hodge and the Princeton faculty came out against them. Princeton's distancing began slowly, but with Nevin's step-by-step attack of Hodge's review of his *Mystical Presence*, the divide became clear, and both camps realized that they were engaged in full-fledged theological warfare. Eventually the combatants formed a truce, but there was no compromise. Years later, Schaff was trusted enough to write for the *Princeton Review*, and Nevin and Hodge corresponded. Still, Nevin remained hurt and made it known in his letters that he believed that Hodge had misrepresented him, and there they left their differences.[1]

Mercersburg and Idealism

Whether by temperament or persuasion, Nevin did not become an idealist overnight. The forces that brought Rauch and Nevin together and led to the replacement of Rauch by Schaff at Mercersburg, were as complex as the forces within the men's own restless spirits. The power of pietism that influenced so many in Germany and America was strong in both Nevin and Schaff. The conversion that overcame them in youth marked them with the indelible print of an evangelical persuasion. The drift of Schaff's maturing into a celebrated representative of orthodox theological science in Germany followed the popular tide of its time.

---

1. Schriver, "Passages in Friendship," 116–22.

Schaff groomed that piety and matched it with a sincere intellectualism approved of and respected by his German colleagues. In contrast, Nevin swam against the current when he embraced idealism, and found small solace among his adoptive denomination. I expect that for Nevin, it was his chagrin at his enemies' failure to see in their former colleague the pious churchman whose immature subjective faith had blossomed in the historic objectivity brought by modern theological science.

Not that Nevin's life was peaceful as an Old School Presbyterian. He was too filled with the moral indignation of a righteous Puritan. He alienated many with his stand against slavery in Pittsburgh,[2] and he had a quick tongue and temper when speaking out on the topics that aroused him. Yet in spite of his theological convictions, he didn't confine himself to a confessional cell. He read widely, in both sacred and secular literature, preferring especially the British Platonists, like Owen,[3] who paved his way to idealism. He was also fascinated with the British romantics, especially Coleridge, and it was in Pittsburgh that Nevin found access to the inspiration behind Coleridge, the German writers.

By 1849 Nevin was so versed in German idealism that he was aggressively engaged in debate over the historical progress of philosophy in Germany, describing the strengths and weaknesses of the writers, and commending the work of the more orthodox mediating school to his readers. His adroitness in the field of philosophy was such that he was able to compose a response to the critical developments that began with Kant. Kant, wrote Nevin, was important for raising the question

---

2. Nevin wrote for *The Friend (of the American Anti-Slavery Society organized in Philadelphia)*, which was a small, literary, and pietistic Christian periodical, published weekly. Nevin eventually accepted the job of editor on behalf of the Young Men's Christian Society (YMCS). The YMCS was an interdenominational organization created to promote evangelical faith in the Pittsburgh area. Nevin used the paper to wage a personal campaign of abolition, arguing in his most controversial article that slavery was a "sin," and that full emancipation of all slaves was a moral imperative. The result of the article was public outrage. Pittsburgh was heavily invested in the slave trade, and Nevin was labeled a threat to the public well-being. Referred to in print as "the most dangerous man in Pittsburgh," Nevin resigned his editorship two years later, even as threats of violence and pressure from the seminary made his departure from Pittsburgh inevitable.

3. Not to be confused with the Cambridge Platonists, these favorite writers of Nevin tended to be from the Puritan movement in England. John Owen (1616–1683) was a deeply spiritual, English Nonconformist and early leader in the development of English Congregationalism.

of the Absolute at a time when rationalism had all but laid God to rest. Kant's elevation of the human will to "full autonomy" allowed access to the unseen world of moral obligation.[4]

Still, Nevin argued that it remained for Hegel to squeeze from Kant much of the rationalism that dogged his system. Nevin believed that Hegel had deflated Kant's inflated system by bringing to earth Kant's high-flying, but essentially empty, "categoric imperative"[sic]. Said Nevin, Hegel was right to argue that an abstract moral law cannot affect life. Likewise, such a law, as recognized by the pure practical reason, as such, had a "formal" character whose nature was to have no particular content. In contrast, Nevin was enthusiastic about Hegel's giving "life" to the so-called universal moral law. Here was no mere principle; it was reason itself, alive with the present "forms of truth and right" operative in the world.[5]

Mercersburg was moving with many in Germany in a philosophical direction that would end traditional dualism and, from their point of view, articulate the overdue, American refutation of common-sense realism. Mercersburg believed that thanks to this modern form of idealism, the will's autonomy and the subsequent recognition of the real world of moral obligation repaired what skepticism had damaged. Hegel's ointment was the speculative insight that what bound the worlds of sight and insight was a "substance" that realists argued could not exist. For realists, reason was an abstraction, a word that described the cooperation of mental faculties. In contrast, idealism regarded reason as a life force, a discrete entity having independent ontological status.

Schaff's work, both early and late, credits Schleiermacher with recovering the Absolute for religion. Indeed, he believed this was theology's God-given assignment: to restore to religion the transcen-

---

4. The argument appears in the previously cited, "'Human Freedom' and 'A Plea for Philosophy.'"

5. Nevin wrote in "Human Freedom," sounding very much like Rauch, "As thus universal and necessary, the being of the law is infinitely real. It is not simply the thought or conception of what is right, not a name merely or mental abstraction representing a certain order of life which men are required to observe; but it is the very forms of truth and right themselves, the absolutely independent power by which they exist in the world" (12). In his unpublished dissertation, "John Williamson Nevin: The Concept of Church Authority, 1844–1858," J. P. Ryan described Nevin's embrace of idealism: "Nevin could view all humanity, in its outward manifestation, as the expression of the Ideal, as the expression of the mind of God that lay behind the visible world" (54).

dental dimension of life and return to men and women the experience of God in human history. Schaff believed that religion entered the world when Adam and Eve left the Garden of Eden. Religion began when permanent damage was done to the relationship of God with God's creation by the human race's purposeful alienation of God through sin. Since then, the role of religion had been the reconciliation of Creator and creatures. For Schaff, rationalism blinded religion to its goal. Idealism recovered the process whereby religion would once again seek the "organic" reconciliation hungered for by both heaven and earth.[6]

Nevin's guarded enthusiasm was just as great for the work of Schleiermacher, perhaps even greater. With Hegel, Schleiermacher had brought intellectual science to its "apex" by recognizing that the whole was more than the sum of the parts: that the concept of "totality" was operative within reality.[7] Common-sense practitioners typically believed that the objects of life and nature and culture produced the concept of totality. On the contrary, argued Schleiermacher, it is "Totality" that produces the objects of life and nature and culture and all reality!

The concept of totality is the substratum of idealist thinking. In order to account for "being," one needs to come to terms with the transcendental dimension of life. For idealists, to settle for a picture of life that simply numbers and divides the objects of experience was to omit a significant part of what constituted reality. Words like "completeness" were not just mental abstractions, coined to enrich language and experience by making a noun out of an adjective, or providing a general description to causally distinct events. Words like "completeness" and "totality" and "wholeness" represent "actual being" in transcendental

---

6. Reflecting the systematic approach of Schleiermacher and the historical genius of Hegel, Schaff produced his *Theological Propaedeutic*. Even as late as this major work, Schaff continued to maintain the position he held in coming to America. He believed that the role of the historian was to understand religion according to the governing principles of organic development. Hence in this particular work, Schaff defined the function of religion, which was to reunite God and human beings (6–17). Much earlier Schaff described that reunion in the person of Jesus. See his *Person of Christ*.

7. Once again, this echoes the romantic theme common to the idealist writers. Schleiermacher's concept of totality was a descendant of Plato's concept of the *Hen* (One).

experience. Said Mercersburg, these states actually exist in reality and are natural aspects of human life.[8]

Of course, the operative term is "organic reconciliation." A host of systems offered to reconcile heaven and earth. Even common-sense realism had drawn its Maginot line, marking off a theological no-man's-land haunted exclusively by the Holy Ghost. For realism, this was a necessary truce, a reconciliation of sorts, between ontologically hostile worlds, negotiated by the Spirit.

Rationalism (the perceived enemy of both idealists and common-sense realists) preferred to divorce the worlds of mind and matter. Materialism went a step further, proposing that what is out of sight should likewise be out of mind (or better, is merely a figment of the mind's imagination). In contrast, idealism sought the reconciliation of mind and body, flesh and spirit, God and creation, and the "fullness" it described included physical union. The unseen world of Spirit must make physical contact with the objects of nature for there to be real, organic union,[9] just as, for example (to cite one of Nevin's favorite analogies), the power that moves the acorn to become the oak must be in physical contact with the acorn.

Idealists' "proofs" were also different. For the most part, they abandoned the inductive proof, unconsciously contributing to the growing criticism of metaphysics. They often conceded the absence of physical evidence, suggesting, instead, that without deducing the unseen force of Spirit, the full description of life was incomplete.

The unseen forces described by the speculative scientists were argued to exist transcendentally. Their proof was by elaborate deduction as it came to expression in phenomenology. They insisted that the forces must exist, or organic development would not be possible. In support of their argument for "absolute being," idealists studied history looking for the seam of organic unfolding that demonstrated the existence of history's purposeful direction and ever-escalating development.

8. Although this is the specific argument of Nevin in his "Human Freedom," the same position is repeated throughout his work and throughout the works of Rauch and Schaff.

9. Nevin uses this analogy frequently, but it comes directly from Rauch. In Rauch's "Ecclesiastical Historiography of Germany," he spoke of the "Idea of the Church" existing in Christ like the parts of one tree. Each part shares its identity with the tree, yet it is distinct (401). The reference to oaks and acorns comes from Rauch's published sermon, "Faith and Reason," 88.

Under F. C. Bauer, Schaff came in contact with Hegel's historical dialectic, recognizing in it the response to rationalism's demythologizing of the Christian faith. The reconciliation of heaven and earth was depicted in the doctrine of the incarnation. But Neander gave Schaff the necessary "last piece" to the puzzle of church history: the incarnate Jesus of history was the organic "first seed" from whom the church, in all of its historical manifestations, would develop.

Likewise, Rauch came by his history through Hegel. Even more than Schaff and Nevin, Rauch described the speculative approach that provided him his critique of American philosophy. In summary, it was as follows: Reason exists independently of reasoning individuals. Yet we who reason are part of the Absolute mind that shares our being. In harmonious cooperation with the senses, reason is completely capable of understanding the world and the laws of nature. When errors or misreason enter in, it is because reason is undone by the passions, which make certain the fallibility of reason.

Passion makes reason especially vulnerable in the areas of religion and morality, where passions are strong. Although reason is directly related to the mind of God (while not identical, as some idealists taught),[10] it is limited to the province of knowledge of the natural world.

Rauch's idealism betrayed the lingering, orthodox tendency to partition the worlds of flesh and spirit. While no ontological rift existed for Rauch, there were phenomenological laws that operated differently in the natural world than in the supernatural world. Reason was master in the first, and the laws that govern reason were dominant. Faith was supreme in the world of spirit, and faith applied the spiritual laws that were exclusive to its domain.

This partition would not have alarmed the majority of American evangelicals to whom Rauch addressed his system. After all, "justification

---

10. This constitutes Rauch's significant departure from Hegel. Philosophically it is characteristic of the mediating approach. Still, it raises critical questions about the integrity of the philosophical foundation as systematic. In strict Hegelian thinking, reason is supreme. In Rauch's "Faith and Reason" (1838), he will only allow reason's supremacy in the realm of nature. Since, with man, all of nature is fallen, reason is also blemished. Thus, Rauch allows latent dualism back into the picture. Still, it is in the qualified sense of a mystery. The spiritual realm is not arrived at by science or reason, but by intuition. The spiritual realm becomes necessary because of a requisite unity or spiritual destination that cannot be supplied except by "faith," and must exist in order for there to be a complete description of life.

by faith alone" was an essential principle of Protestant religion. However, Rauch's replacing reason as the meditating concept for natural knowledge over faculty psychology's "sense experience" was unacceptable to Rauch's American, evangelical audience, and realist disapproval was unanimous. Again, reason was simply a general term, not a thing in itself.

Still, Rauch was engaged in Christian apologetics as much as he was a salesman for German idealism. Orthodoxy was under the gun from rationalists, disenchanted scientists, and social critics all demanding solid empirical evidence for the claims of religion. Rauch's speculative science offered this solution: reason, not sense experience, is the source of knowledge of the world, and when reason is applied to disprove the claims of religion, it is misapplied. While reason is the "highest gift" we own in the natural world, it is not authoritative for the state of grace where faith reigns over the necessary information for our access to heaven.[11]

In Rauch's evangelical idealism, he believed he had corralled realism's tendency toward deism and skepticism. This, of course, was common among idealists of all stripes in his era. Although he shared with realism the anthropomorphic starting point, Rauch's psychology provided evidence that reason could be apprehended within individual consciousness. The unity of consciousness is also the ground for the essential unity of faith and reason, such that they exist harmoniously, in full sympathy with their inherited domains. Starting rationally, reason supplies knowledge of the natural world that must lead to the desire for knowledge of the spiritual world. Starting spiritually, faith supplies knowledge of the spiritual world that must then lead to the desire for knowledge of the natural world. Thus reason, argued Rauch, supplies the "force" of the argument for the existence of the spiritual world. Not that reason can supply religious knowledge. It can, however, infer from the organic structure of the universe a world not apprehended by the senses.

Rauch conceives an "end" or purpose operative in life as an organizing principle, but also as a "force" moving things in a preordained

---

11. Rauch's departure from Hegel becomes glaringly obvious in the following sentence from his, "Faith and Reason." In describing the experience whereby reason perceives the invisible world, he writes, "From this phenomena [sic] we conclude upon the power itself, though our own senses cannot perceive it, nor reason demonstrate it. Here, then, begins the sphere of faith—not of the faith of the Christian but of common faith" (88). This is also the argument of his *Inner Life of the Christian*, 18–19.

direction. This power is unseen. It brings vegetable life from seed to blossom, animal life from conception to maturity, and it controls the movement of history and morality from disunity to unity in an ever-ascending, law-abiding course. However, Rauch did not imply that reason apprehends these forces itself. It merely apprehends the existence of the order or organization of matter into higher levels of being. In effect, reason merely apprehends the absence of evidence of a spiritual world. Reason merely supplies evidence that something necessary for understanding the organic unity of life is beyond rational inquiry. Reason cannot supply the "form" of organic objects.

Only faith can provide the invisible world suspected by reason. Interestingly, Rauch calls this kind of faith "common faith,"[12] which exists in us all, as portal to the "sphere of faith." But, without Christian conviction, common faith waits at faith's threshold. There, it simply longs for transcendental experience, expressing its desire for "fulfillment." It is the common provocation to heightened awareness that often leads to restlessness. In this, the individual can recognize a common impulse driving him or her to a certain end. The desired "completeness" envisioned by the individual, said Rauch, is a universal longing of the soul to find eternal contentment, or simply put, to reach heaven. As we recognize the existence of common faith, we are open to suspect the existence of an entire world of unseen forces. Yet knowledge of that world depends on the Holy Spirit, for this realm is owned by Christian religion.[13]

---

12. This question was at the heart of the nature/grace controversy within Roman Catholicism in the middle part of the twentieth century. Much of it was simply a dispute over the right interpretation of St. Thomas Aquinas's understanding of *capax gratiae*; but more than that, it signaled a major division in Roman Catholic theology. That division was centered in dualism, namely the degree to which the worlds of spirit and nature are divided, with theologians like Henri de Lubac seeking to lessen the rift. Likewise the issue remains controversial in Wolfhart Pannenberg's, *Systematic Theology*, where a similar idea of "common faith" encourages dualism in poststructuralist theology. Pannenberg allows the possibility of a natural knowledge of God in a way that is similar to Rauch. Such knowledge is not gained by reason so much as it comes by way of intuition. His method is to understand that capacity in terms of our *cognitio Dei naturalis insita*, rather than the traditional *cognitio Dei naturalis acquisita*.

13. That Christianity was the pinnacle of religion was the conclusion of Schelling, Hegel, and Schleiermacher. The mediating school focused on the "principle of incarnation" but went further by making the historical Jesus, and not simply the idea of Jesus, the source of that principle. That was a clear departure from their teachers.

Idealism in America

Nevin believed Rauch's philosophic work to be, perhaps, the most innovative in America.[14] Rauch schooled Americans in the "contemporary problem" and so labored to bring America into the modern theological world. He felt that the previous scientific age's gifts and its hidden dangers needed to be exposed (the fuller implications of the "Enlightenment" were still emerging), and so he led the Mercersburg movement in the belief that America needed to mature and take its place with Europe in wrestling with the historical forces that controlled all of life.

Princeton, along with the new evangelicals and revivalists, took another view. Princeton wanted to preserve the unique American experience, believing it offered the means to true Christian faith. Revivalists were just as certain of the verity of their beliefs, but they were innovators, anxious to import their insights abroad. Neither Princeton nor the revivalists felt the need to embrace the changes brought to orthodoxy by intellectual Europe, or to worry much about the historic source of their confessional stance. Instead, they were equally skeptical of the European experience, and would simply export their dogmas with missionary zeal.

Even today it is rare that evangelicals would subject revelation, or the supernatural contents of their faith, to rigorous rational inquiry, especially as Mercersburg would have it, on a global scale. Mercersburg saw the problem as a human problem requiring a cooperative solution. Still, most American evangelicals, including Mercersburg, overrated America's religious significance (as contemporary American evangelicals still do). They earnestly believed America to be the next (maybe the final) "testing ground" for modern religion, and many felt that the success of this test depended on the diligence of all faithful souls.[15]

14. Nevin believed Rauch had supplied a new, middle path between the Scottish and German systems. In his review of Rauch's, *Psychology*, Nevin wrote, "Such a work too, well executed, may be expected to answer a most important practical purpose, in counteracting and correcting the *onesidedness* of both these antagonistic tendencies of the time . . . and reconciling and bringing together what there may be in them separately of truth and right" (n.p.).

15. Many evangelicals believed America to be the "New Jerusalem," where true religion had, at last, found its home. Its leaders were deified as saints and religious icons. From this perception there arose the mingling of Continental Christianity with American patriotism resulting in an approach to Christianity in which American

Thus, in Rauch, Nevin found a philosopher addressing the most important questions of the age, and throughout his life he would echo many of Rauch's philosophical themes. For Rauch, Nevin, and Schaff, the philosophical watershed was the unity of faith and reason. Idealism embraced the mind as "substance." This insight was pivotal. At idealism's core is the idea that "nature exists only for mind," and Nevin never relinquished this fundamental axiom.[16] For Mercersburg, absolute causality operating in history revealed the mind's dominance over the world that can be seen. Mind provided the organizing principle wherein life has direction and identity. As John Woolverton observed of Nevin, "in true Hegelian fashion, the Christian absolute was everywhere becoming increasingly visible as a higher plane of spiritual synthesis was achieved."[17]

---

values became confused with Christian values, and the unfolding kingdom of God was the course of American history. American mainline Protestant religion still contains much of this at its heart. For an edifying account of this, see Albanese, *Sons of the Fathers: The Civil Religion of the American Revolution*. On the topic of the scarcity of critical evangelical thought, see Noll, *Scandal of the Evangelical Mind*. Noll begins his book: "The scandal of the evangelical mind is that there is not much of an evangelical mind" (3). Enough said.

16. Nevin was severely criticized by Orestes Brownson, the brilliant convert to Roman Catholicism, for his avowed idealism. Brownson (1803–1876) was a member of America's transcendentalist movement before becoming a formidable spokesman for the Roman Catholic Church. Nevin was unrepentant in his replies to Brownson, rejecting Brownson's arguments by suggesting that Brownson had understandably reached a dead end in Unitarianism's heretical reaction to Puritan religion. Brownson, said Nevin, should realize his was a position supported by a philosophy ill-equipped to defend his adoptive denomination's convictions in an age of scientific discovery. However, instead of turning to modern, German theology, where Christian apologetics commenced, Brownson hid in the dark and undignified dogma of medieval Catholicism. Thus, he had exchanged one form of rationalism for another. Failing to find meaning in a church that made logical sense, he embraced a church that simply established that sense in its outward form. For one of Nevin's clearest descriptions of the mind's place and power, see his literary debate with Brownson, published in *Brownson's Quarterly Review*, Vols. 1–3 (1844–1858) and in *The Mercersburg Review*, as "Brownson's Quarterly Review" and "Brownson's Review Again," Vol. 2 (1850).

17. John Woolverton was the astute, modern Anglican critic of Mercersburg, who has done so much to acquaint readers with the brilliant debates of Nevin with Episcopalians. Fascinating reading is found in Nevin's literary debate with the Oxford fellow and influential tractarian, Robert Isaac Wilberforce (1802–1857), second son of William Wilberforce. Many readers will find the debate with Wilberforce interesting for the fame achieved by the English controversialist and eventual convert to Roman Catholicism. It was published in *The Mercersburg Review*, 2 (1850) as "Wilberforce On

In summary, the philosophical goal of Mercersburg was to establish Christianity's reasonability in an age dominated by rationalistic doubt. The banner under which they struggled was the metaphor of "organic union." For Mercersburg, organic union established the necessary link between this world and the next in the person of Jesus Christ. It was a link mediated by reason where, by faith, reason understood the need for a transcendental experience of the supernatural world. In contrast to the many evangelicals who called for "revival," Mercersburg's call was for the "right of Christians to be supernaturalists."[18]

Mercersburg was hard to ignore even though they resisted the popular tide by speaking out against revivalism. Their academic credentials were impressive. Clearly the lion's share of their credibility came from their innovative work in church history and theology. No American institution could rival Mercersburg for the level of sophistication in historical theory and research, and Mercersburg applied that level of sophistication to the task of unmasking the "real" source of rationalism as they had received it from the mediating school. They believed with the mediating school that the current source of rationalism was the preoccupation with the formal principle that gave itself over to unlicensed subjectivity. In America that problem seemed especially dangerous. In order to recover the balance and to return the church to its proper historical path, Mercersburg felt it needed to promote the material principle that stressed the living presence of Christ in the institutional church. They argued that the restoration of balance would instill a faith that did not simply "justify" the believer, but also "assure" the believer, giving the believer the confidence to overcome rationalistic doubt.

So it was that German speculative theology provided Mercersburg the phenomenological and historical insights to develop their own brand of supernatural theology that would issue in an American, churchly evangelicalism ("evangelical catholicism"). In the speculative idealism

---

the Incarnation." However, there is much more substance in Nevin's late-1870s debate with the American bishop, Arthur Coxe. The quote above appeared in Woolverton's article, "Nineteenth-Century Ecclesiology: J. W. Nevin and the Episcopalians," 367.

18. While the well-known reaction to revivalism by Mercersburg was a return to the historical church and its sacraments and confessions, still Mercersburg's philosophic defense of a "supernatural faith" was all consuming. Nevin pressed it beyond the place of the great American theologian Horace Bushnell (1802–1876). For Bushnell's perspective, see his *Nature and the Supernatural* (1858). For Nevin's response, see "Natural and Supernatural," for his review of the same.

of Germany, Mercersburg found a philosophy bold enough to reveal the "interior fundamental form of the world's life," and with romantic fervor, Mercersburg shared the idealists' grand scheme: to believe that such a philosophy would develop the consciousness *of the entire world*. All that was required was an adjustment to that philosophy, in order to bring it into line, so that it could understand its full purpose and so transform humanity into the complete "image of God."[19]

Mercersburg's Adjustment

In spite of sharing with German idealism the project of developing a religious language that could reasonably articulate the Christian experience of God's participation in human history, Mercersburg departed from Hegel and Schleiermacher on a number of issues, and in the area of ecclesiology they made their most significant departure from the speculative approach. In the case of Hegel, they broke ranks by placing theology above philosophy, reversing his vision of religious belief coming to its full historical expression in speculative science. Mercersburg testified in print that philosophy was merely a tool of theology. Covertly, they hinted at that prejudice by omitting any comprehensive critique of the philosopher's system. Rather, they simply concluded that philosophy's job was to translate thinking into evangelical faith.

Schleiermacher would not have disagreed with the latter conclusion, but where he and Hegel would have held no quarter with Mercersburg (and many from the mediating school) was the way Mercersburg replaced idealism's emphasis on the idea of Christ with the actual, historical person of Christ (as believed by orthodox tradition). The believer didn't so much rise into a higher level of God-consciousness made possible by Christ (as depicted in Schleiermacher's system), but became unified with the whole person of Christ. And their acceptance of the more Hebraic, material language of tradition, which

---

19. In these ambitious claims, Mercersburg revealed its romantic stripe and once again demonstrated its kinship with German idealism through the mediating approach. Nevin's bold claim appeared in his treatise, "Human Freedom," 40. Nevin accused Bushnell of a view of the supernatural that depicted the activity of God in the world as a theophany in the style of the Old Testament rather than as in the organic view that saw supernatural faith as harmoniously linked to our experience of nature. Therefore, said Nevin, the supernatural could not be treated as a "transient phenomenon" as Bushnell left it.

endorsed the ontological existence of evil and sin, was blatantly absent in both Hegel and Schleiermacher.

According to Mercersburg, this was an unacceptable apostasy in German idealism, and it revealed to them a tragic misreading of human psychology and experience (not to mention biblical teaching).[20] Sadly, for the logical consistency of the idealist system, it was not enough to simply return the doctrine of sin to its traditional place in Western theology. When Mercersburg (along with other mediating theologians) opted for the Augustinian concept of evil, they disrupted the monism fundamental to Hegel's system that made God's participation in the world both natural and rational.

In preferring Augustine, many in the mediating school returned evil and the realm of sin to a place beyond history. It was no longer a mere moment within the movement of the Spirit (*Geist*). The preference was significant. The direction of German idealism had been that under no circumstances could the existence of evil fit a rational explanation unless both good and evil were different moments of the same spirit: the particulars of figurative thought and the practical effects of moral decision making. The obvious question plagued traditional views and begged the question, if evil had some independent power, to what end was it motivated? The conundrum of theodicy once again reared its head.

Vice versa, idealism recognized the force of theological necessity. Augustine needed for evil to come to full expression in the concept of antagonism to the good. The force and full expression of that antagonism would naturally lead to an entity as malevolent as Satan, whose presence and influence in a fallen and corrupted will might easily find a

---

20. Their christocentrism united the mediators, but it naturally raised the question of why the incarnation was necessary. The idealist philosophers understood sin as a natural and unavoidable part of being human. Hegel believed there could be no good without bad. Schleiermacher believed that sin was tied to humanity's sensuous nature. Mercersburg realized that the idealists sought an explanation of sin that made reasonable sense of Christian claims: What sense is there in arguing, as church tradition had for centuries argued, that humanity's folly brought about the incarnation; that sin made the incarnation necessary? Yet any attempt to explain the incarnation outside of the recognition of human falleness and the ontological existence of evil resulted in an inadequate explanation of the "highest act of God's love." For a fuller discussion of this, see Nevin's "Cur Deus Homo?"

welcome if not a happy home deep in the recesses of the human heart.[21] Still, idealists maintained that the *raison d'être* of evil is the corruption of humanity, which is to have no being outside of humanity's being, on whom the reality of evil depends.

Evil was much too serious business to evangelicals to seemingly lessen its force by simply contrasting it with good. To them, such a view could never understand the power of darkness, nor could it ever muster enough courage or sense to stand against evil—once and for all. Furthermore, Mercersburg was more interested in preserving the church's confession than preserving philosophic rigor. Again, for them, Hegel and Schleiermacher's systematic consistency remained captive to the very rationalism idealism sought to dispel.[22] Just as rationalism balked at the thought of miracles, it filed down the sharpness of the doctrine of sin and so removed its cutting edge. Mankind's depravity was one Calvinist tenet they would not adjust.[23] Sin and miracles embarrassed rationalists, but they confused idealists. Mercersburg would have its idealism wed to a supernaturalism that preserved orthodoxy. Sin made it necessary that God become directly involved in human history as a uniquely supernatural act.

There were other areas of disagreement, and Mercersburg benefited from the idealists' own criticisms of their colleagues. With Hegel, Mercersburg declared Schleiermacher's rooting religion in subject experience as weak. In Schleiermacher's subjectivism the church foundered as a loose confederation of like-minded people, sharing the experience of the divine. The criticism was that with Schleiermacher the church

21. For Augustine, the devil's existence is not "evil *qua* existence." Likewise, succumbing to temptation in order for it to be sin must be willful. See Augustine's "On True Religion," xiii, 26–xiv, 27, *Augustine: Earlier Writings*.

22. Mercersburg was convinced that the systems of Hegel and Schleiermacher were devoutly Christian. They concluded that their errors derived from rationalism's decades-long grip on Prussian religious life. In idealism's effort to free Germans from that grip, they were unable to entirely disentangle themselves from rationalism's penchant for formalism. Likewise, Mercersburg believed that Hegel's emphasis of Spirit (the inward or unseen), robbed faith of objectivity, suggesting to them a lack of courage in Hegel to stand firm on behalf of the supernatural.

23. In John T. McNeill's masterful edition of Calvin's *Institutes* (1.1.1, Sec. 3), there is a revealing footnote describing Calvin's different uses of the term "nature," followed by the observation, "This distinction is indispensable for understanding the relation of God to creation and to sin as well as the precise sense in which a doctrine of 'total' depravity may be attributed to Calvin." (McNeil, 38).

never becomes a historical institution or social form. Schleiermacher's subjectivity insisted that the church remain independent of the state and focused exclusively on the redemption of fallen humanity.[24] Mercersburg's confessional and ecclesiastical emphases made it essential that faith come to expression in the institutional church.

Mercersburg turned the lessons of the mediating school and Schelling's new philosophy against Hegel. Suspicion of Hegel's lingering rationalism implied to Nevin and Schaff that his system might lead to skepticism concerning the supernatural world and, hence, to a potential philosophical imbalance towards objectivity. Nevin argued that even with his sublimation of the real into the ideal, Hegel had a fetish for the material world. Said Nevin, Hegel's philosophy makes "the idea the mistress of the fact."[25] Here Schelling's critical influence is obvious.

In contrast, Mercersburg's orthodox idealism gave greater weight to the idea. In effect, Mercersburg followed Rauch's lead in assigning to the ideal world natural and supernatural qualities. The form of the natural world was itself natural and constantly coming into expression in everyday life. The supernatural qualities and entities inhabiting the ideal world made only rare appearances in the natural world, and could only be apprehended and comprehended by faith. This constitutes a serious and totally irreconcilable reversal of the Hegelian system.

Mercersburg argued that philosophy must move beyond the merely physical and recognize the superior place and power of the ideal over the actual. That which brings meaning to life, giving it its eternal quality, comes through the ideal. Indeed, in order for there to be "true philosophy," the Absolute must have ascendancy over all that is "simply empirical and particular."[26] The ascendancy of the Absolute and the

---

24. In his famous, *Speeches*, Schleiermacher wrote: "The state pollutes religious fellowship by introducing into its deepest mysteries its own interests." A few paragraphs later, he wrote, "Away then with every such union between church and state!"(123–25). This should not suggest, however, that Mercersburg advocated state religion.

25. Nevin made this statement quite early on, indeed, when he first wrote for *The Weekly Messenger of the German Reformed Church* (No. 40, 1848). Later he would share with Schaff the more mature criticism that Hegel's system allowed the church to develop indiscriminately. To Mercersburg, the church in Germany was looking more and more like the state. The Mercersburg professors, along with a host of mediating theologians, held to a concept, present in Schelling, that the Church was prefigured in Christ, to the extent that its development could never sublimate Christ, nor could the church ever "transcend itself" in the way suggested by Rothe.

26. The terms and argument are from Nevin's "Plea for Philosophy," 36. However,

power of the ideal over the real identified Mercersburg with Schelling, who provided Schaff with his philosophical criticism of Hegel.

Schelling believed that Hegel's dialectic was fundamentally objective, describing the phenomenon of thought coming into being in the natural world. The problem, objected Schelling, was that Hegel was really a materialist who had not effectively demonstrated how thought translates into matter. Schelling claimed that, in effect, Hegel's science was one of hindsight, and that the result was an arbitrary dialectic whereby cultural and historical manifestations are fit into a Procrustean scheme that offered no vision of the future and an artificially constructed past.

Hegel's insistence that the ideal come to expression in the real suggested, in Mercersburg's thinking, the complete identification of the "divine Church" with its historical manifestation. Hegel had always insisted, in contrast to Schleiermacher, that the church was an organ of the state, whose purpose was the redemption of its citizens.[27] Mercersburg concluded that the implications of Hegel's "fixed idea" culminated in the frightening conclusions of Hegel's successor, Rothe. Said Mercersburg, Rothe took Hegel a step further, openly violating the "organic principle." In Rothe, the state swallowed up the church by assuming its institutional role.

Mercersburg bristled at the notion of the church losing its identity to the state. To them, this was the insidious outcome of a philosophy that made a "principle" (the fixed idea) the absolute standard for determining history. Invoking the later Schelling, Mercersburg argued that Hegel had transgressed his own concept of inward, organic unity by making the Christian faith "transcend" the original idea of the church established in history by Christ. They insisted that while the church can manifest itself in a variety of historic forms, it cannot transform itself or be transformed from the fundamental character given it by Christ.[28]

---

it must be pointed out that here that Nevin is arguing with common-sense realists and not with German idealists. Still, his emphasis of the Absolute would not have changed if he had been arguing with Hegelians, as demonstrated by his and Schaff's identification with Schelling.

27. While this is a widely held view, James Yerkes, in his *Christology of Hegel*, describes Hegel's system as one of checks and balances that understands church and state as complementary of one another.

28. This was a difficult tightrope to walk. Mercersburg rejected Hegel's objective conceptual model but also pietism's appeal to subjective inspiration. Mercersburg struggled for balance by replacing existing conceptual models. Asserting the unmediated,

Schaff came to this conclusion while studying with Baur in Tübigen. Where Baur shared Hegel's more liberal views, Schaff began to distance himself from his celebrated teacher. Baur followed Hegel's dialectical triad where historical progress was a series of "negations" into higher stages of development. Each new "synthesis" was a transformation. This was unacceptable to Schaff, who remained true to a confessional interpretation of the church's development. Schaff would later turn to Schelling to provide himself with an unchanging idea in the organic process of historical development.

However, while Schelling provided the acceptable philosophical rationale, Mercersburg did not feel obligated to "prove" their position philosophically. In this they followed the lead of Rauch. Although logic and science must be applied to the question of the church's historic evolution, ultimately understanding the nature of the church required a confessional prism and the rule of faith.

Because the church provides exclusive insight into the fullest understanding of reality, reasoning outside of faith is flawed. Participation in a supersensual existence by faith provides access to both worlds. Nevin called this the "world of idea." It is a world exclusive to Christians dwelling in the sphere of grace. As Nevin developed his theology, he went beyond Schaff in describing the way in which Christians have access to this special world.[29] Still, both scholars stressed the importance of the church as the repository of the word and sacraments. Likewise they emphasized the material principles operative in the word and sacraments, insisting that the word (Christ) became flesh. They agreed that the sacraments provide the means by which the believer can be united with the flesh of Christ. The mystical state of grace that provides the Christian access to the unseen world of Spirit springs from the unity of Christ and the believer.

As Nevin studied Cyprian, immersing himself in the material principle, and suspecting even the mediating school of not having rid

---

real presence of Christ in the church restricted gross materialism. Subjectivity was curtailed by appeals to Scripture and ecclesiastical tradition. Schaff's view of this is detailed in his "Modern Christianity" in *History of the Christian Church*.

29. This is clearly evident in Nevin's articles on Cyprian but is most fully developed in his controversy with Dorner. In his articles on Cyprian, Nevin begins to wed his Christology to symbolics. Ultimately Nevin will make faith as articulated by the confession (specifically the Apostles' Creed), the objective source of faith.

itself of rationalism's imbalance that listed toward the "formal principle," he began to argue that Christian reasoning depends on creed and confession—that entrance into the world of spirit transforms one's thinking process. Indeed, all "real" knowledge, said Nevin, begins with the state of grace mystically supplied in union with the humanity of Christ provided by the church.[30]

Linking the believing individual to Christ's humanity was provocative for American evangelicals. It was at the point of corporeal contact with the divine that even Schaff began to distance himself from Nevin. In principle, Schaff agreed that union with Christ was union with Christ's humanity. It was agreed that this was necessary to establish "real" union. But Nevin began to interpret physical union in a way that went beyond the mediating school.

Nevin believed that Eucharist marked the avenue of access to God, suggesting even to those who had been previously sympathetic to Nevin's views a lowering of the importance of the "word of God" (Scripture). In Eucharist, material contact provided the grounds for relationship with the source of spiritual knowledge, i.e., Jesus Christ. The response to the presence of Christ demanded a confession, perfectly summarized for Nevin in the Apostles' Creed. For him, the Creed became more than a human response to the person of Christ. The Creed had the power of faith itself. It revealed the very nature of the divine Son of God, as the faithful experienced his life in a shared, spoken confession.

That supernatural relationship, as confession, became the faith of the Creed. Nevin maintained that it was the source of unity for Christians for nearly two thousand years, and it was exclusively available through the church. Without the church, there simply was no access to God in Jesus Christ.[31] At that point, Schaff disagreed. Schaff would not place as much stress on the creeds, thinking it might weaken the place of Scripture in orthodox Protestant theology.

---

30. In what became the only significant departure from his colleague, Philip Schaff, Nevin wrote in his "Answer to Professor Dorner": "To believe now in such an organic power of redemption, the actual presence in the world of a constitution of grace no less real than the constitution of man's fallen life on the outside of it; to believe in this as the result of Christ's victory over sin and death, the fruit of His resurrection, and the form of his presence working in the world through the Spirit to the end of time; to believe in all this, I say, is to believe what is substantially the article of the Holy Catholic Church in the Creed" (579).

31. See Nevin's, "Answer to Professor Dorner."

At the outset Mercersburg had wide support in the German Reformed Church. Slowly that support began to erode until there was a well-established anti-Mercersburg movement within the denomination. Once again, Mercersburg was battling on two fronts. Initially, it was a simple matter dealing with the small but vehement protest within the denomination. Nevertheless, American hostility to the Mercersburg agenda was seething beneath evangelical protectionism and fierce hatred of Roman Catholicism, and no one was more protective of America's Protestant orthodoxy than the professors at Princeton Seminary.

As antagonism outside the denomination grew, criticism within became more credible and widespread. With Princeton's support, the anti-Mercersburg forces became formidable, heightening the sense of urgency and firming each side's resolve.

It is of considerable interest that Dr. Hodge postponed work on his system of realistic dualism to participate in the debates with Nevin sparked by *The Mystical Presence* (1846). Ironically, it wasn't until a year after its publication that Hodge launched his attack. We can only speculate at the reasons for the delay and suggest that Princeton was in a state of shock that the battle for America's conscience had shifted from the mildly irritating problem of revivals and Arminianism to the greater threat of infidelity and pantheism brought by German idealism. Hodge literally put off his production of realistic dualism (or, at least, deferred work on his *Systematic Theology*) to lead in the attack against what became a consuming interest: the eradication of the Mercersburg theology, and with it its friendly disposition toward the Roman Catholic religion.[32]

America's Response to Speculative Theology

When Rauch's *Psychology* appeared in 1840, it was reviewed by those brave enough to venture into the unfamiliar waters of German philosophy. Nevin was the only reviewer favorably disposed. Princeton's response was the majority view. They pursued a path of detached

---

32. It was with considerable vagueness that Hodge couches apologies for his late review. It was most likely that he had to be urged to write the review. Furthermore, in effect, what Hodge postponed was his developing lectures that would become his *Systematic Theology*. In spite of Hodge's personal reluctance to take up debate with Nevin, his commitment to the refutation of German idealism and the Mercersburg theology is well documented.

collegiality, reminding their readers how refreshing it was to have the complexities of the German system explained to them by a pious familiar writing in their language. Other writers, those with nothing personal at stake, panned the work.

At Harvard Francis Bowen found the book so unfamiliar that he was hesitant to comment.[33] Nevin reported that New Haven's Dr. Murdock fared no better. Rauch's approach was so unique that Murdock was left with only the single impression that the young German idealist was a "pantheist" out of the Hegelian school. The general conclusion was that the *Psychology* was "a wholly un-Christian book."[34]

American evangelicals were not angry with Rauch so much as they were dismayed that he would import German idealism to America. Their impression was that this new methodology was a threat to orthodoxy, and that it would only confuse American readers. The *Puritan Recorder*, ordinarily in supreme opposition to the sentiments expressed by *Brownson's Quarterly Review*, joined chorus in denouncing what they believed was German idealism's speculative non-sense.

In the same vein but much later, Princeton, rising to the threat that Mercersburg posed to their approach six years after the death of Rauch, reviewed Schaff's *What Is Church History?* warning readers of the outlandish theories of German historians. The reviewer, J. Addison Alexander, encouraged the reader to use "common sense" in rejecting the "refuse" within its pages while applying the "wholesome" product. Alexander commented:

> If all the teeming German minds now striving, like the wise men of Laputa, to extract sunbeams out of cucumbers, could be engaged by some great impulse in historical researches, we should gain a treasure of imperishable knowledge, and lose what? The next stage of Hegelianismus.[35]

Alexander wasn't attacking Schaff so much as German speculative philosophy, and especially the speculative idealists' pet concept of "organic growth." Said Alexander, the idea is Newman's, and betrays his historical apologies for the corrupt Roman Catholic Church.

---

33. Bowen, Review of *Psychology*, 385–88.
34. Nevin, "Philosophy of Dr. Rauch," 419.
35. Alexander, "Historical Theology," review of *What Is Church History?* 94.

Ultimately, it was Princeton who intensified the most violent reaction to Mercersburg by directly tying German idealism to pantheism and to Roman Catholic practice or sympathy. While the connections were unjustified, the effect was enormous. Given the enormous influence of Princeton, denominational leaders and theologians were tempted to perceive Mercersburg just as Princeton portrayed them, which boiled down to "pantheistic," Roman Catholic sympathizers.[36]

Ironically, the most caustic supporters of the Princeton viewpoint were not Presbyterians at all, but a small, extremely vocal group of dissidents within the German Reformed Church. One of their leaders, Samuel Helfenstein, described the psychological theories of Mercersburg as "unintelligible, like their theology," and filled with Roman "superstition."[37] When the denomination wholeheartedly accepted Schaff's *Principle of Protestantism*, Joseph Berg, another outspoken leader of the opposition, wrote that the German Reformed Church had welcomed "the most odious system of error and superstition which has ever afflicted the world." That system was essentially the faith and practice of the Roman Catholic Church. Berg argued that in approving Schaff's book, the denomination replaced its own confessional position, which made Scripture authoritative, and installed the Roman Catholic Church as the "final judge of controversies."[38]

Berg joined with the majority of the Mercersburg critics to denounce evangelical catholicism calling it the brainchild of deceived men. Furthermore, he said, the philosophical Pied Piper whose theories led Mercersburg down the primrose path was none other than Hegel, whose "vain babblings" lead to pantheism, and whose influence on German philosophy left it unfit for the "evangelical mind."

Now, claimed Berg, Hegel's disciples at Mercersburg are propagating an idea of history so inconceivable as to convince him that "the author's mind is deplorably warped by vain speculations." Berg cautioned his readers to regard those ideas with "feelings of deep aversion and distrust," and to disregard entirely, as false and pernicious, the concept of historical development as an organic process.[39]

36. To some extent this could be expected, considering the breadth and influence of Hodge's *Princeton Review*.
37. Helfenstein, "Mercersburg Controversy."
38. Berg, "Mercersburg Theology," 75–77.
39. Berg, "German Controversy," 306–7.

Even the ordinarily gentle Taylor Lewis, of the sister Dutch Reformed Church (Reformed Church in America), admitted that most Americans would never accept the Mercersburg position on the history of the church. Although he welcomed the historical research that repudiated the popular idea of Protestantism as descending directly from underground Waldenses, he would not accept any position that identified the true church of Christ with the Roman Catholic Church. Lewis wrote that the papal line could not contain the "true vitality of Christ's mystical body." Finally, he concluded that while "this semi-Pagan, semi-atheistic monstrosity" was somehow in the church, it was never "the Church."[40]

Lewis respected Schaff's historical science enough to grant him the point that Protestant religion developed in reaction to and therefore was a product of Roman Catholicism. Likewise, Lewis saw a great deal wrong with America's sectarianism and its ultra-Protestant tendencies, which, he said, threatened to further disunite the "one body of Christ." Still, Lewis was unwilling to grant what he believed to be Mercersburg's request for an outright rejection of the traditional American Protestant faith. Lewis remained convinced, in spite of Mercersburg's vehement arguments to the contrary, that "a real church feeling" still existed in Protestant America, and while he acknowledged that that feeling was disrupted by "criminal sectarianism," the solution would not be found in the idea of "real union to Christ's humanity" as offered by Mercersburg.

Lewis reflected the national mood when he preferred the traditional evangelical dispensation that harmonizes heaven and earth, where the mingling of "un-alikes" was relatively rare. In the salvific act, according to Lewis, the Holy Spirit provided access to the body of Christ. Said Lewis, Mercersburg would have a great deal more success if they sought to convince Protestants that the importance of the Eucharist was, indeed, in its unifying effect. But, cautioned Lewis, in contrast to Mercersburg, that effect was in unifying the individual believer with Christ's "human soul" rather than with Christ's humanity.

Few outside the Mercersburg circle were as sympathetic as Lewis. The American reaction to German idealism provided but one example of America's growing resolve (or at least evangelical resolve

40. Lewis, "Church Question," 79–80.

and Princeton's resolve) to establish a singular identity and to violently resist any new invasion from beyond her boarders.

The upheavals in Europe contributed to this, but so did America's growing sense of independence. Even more recently, German idealism could be dismissed with the suggestion that it is obscure. William Carlough puzzled, as late as 1962, over the mystery of how Nevin's theology could be as penetrating as it was, considering his dependence on German idealism.[41] Likewise, Mark Noll, one of evangelical theology's modern representatives, observed that Mercersburg's reaction to revival theology included an assault on evangelical philosophy. Said Noll, that philosophy was handed down by Locke and Edwards and graciously received at Princeton, where it was modified and enriched by Hodge and others. It was a philosophy indebted to Scottish common-sense realism, whose penchant for practical solutions and pragmatic answers (in effect, the answers that work) best fit the American way of life. Noll's observations strike an ominous chord, for he finds that evangelicals were better suited to the American context, as their obvious numerical success testified.[42]

Noll recognizes that in Hodge, evangelicals celebrated a key architect of their system of faith. Not that Hodge was a revivalist. In fact he supported the Old School cause, which was losing ground to revivalist fervor. Moreover, after the Civil War many new currents would develop within the Calvinist churches, and sharp confessional identity would slip even further. Still, Hodge's outline of the American evangelical faith's most basic philosophical and religious presuppositions would remain fundamentally intact to the present day. Indeed they continue to buttress the "Christian Right's" dogmatic lock on orthodoxy, enshrining the "embattled fortress" mentality of Hodge and Princeton. Certainly no one fought harder than Princeton to preserve these presuppositions

---

41. Carlough, "German Idealism and the Theology of John W. Nevin."

42. Noll's work is remarkable for its historical appreciation of the issues that originally separated America's evangelicals into the traditional and now fading "mainline" camp and the growing, independent-church camp, which most recently has made political headlines in the Christian Right. He recognizes Princeton and the work of Hodge as fundamental for understanding the beginnings of evangelical independence and conservative religion in America. His article "What Has Wheaton To Do With Jerusalem: Lessons from Evangelicals for the Reformed," 8–15, might be considered seminal for the way his "lessons" have been applied.

from attack, and the battle plan featured Hodge as the most capable critic of Mercersburg's introducing German idealism to America.

In part Hodge's criticism sprang from his canonization of realist thinking. In American common-sense realism, Hodge enjoyed what he believed was a sound, down-to-earth perspective. It seemed to him plainspoken and candid. It concerned itself with the practical matters of human experience. He liked the way it recognized its own limits, expressing a healthy dependence on what God might supply when human ingenuity failed. What a contrast to German idealism!

Hodge was immediately suspicious of the so-called new learning imported from Germany. He identified in it the very same rationalistic bent found in Strauss. Its skeptical coolness demythologized and so deflated the very same canon he was raising to new heights. Idealism, like its parent rationalism, questioned the reliability of the texts that he was giving prominence to. It humanized Christ, and so, in his mind, marginalized him. Ultimately (and quite late in his debate with Mercersburg), Hodge came to appreciate the difference between rationalism and idealism, and he finally accepted that the mediating school developed in reaction to the work of Hegel and Schleiermacher. But Hodge believed that the students of Schleiermacher and Hegel remained remorseless idealists who refused to repent of their affection for rationalism.

For these American critics, in idealism's romantic and "typically German" (translate "extreme") reaction to rationalism, it had leaped clear over from hating God to making itself God. But more than anything else, all this romantic exuberance issued in a pompous and overstated religious language, without a care for practical matters. Nor did it demonstrate the least little interest in making itself intelligible to non-Germans.

For Hodge, German idealism wasn't simply a new development in philosophy; it reeked of intellectual elitism. Its pronouncements were clad in imperious language that mocked the American experience. Hidden in its lofty phraseology was the implication that American thinking was incomplete and in need of enlightenment. But Hodge was not surprised by this development. He recognized a distinct difference in German thinking.

He called it the "natural obscurity of the German mind."[43] As this threat to American "plain thinking" grew from a distant one, as having an impact exclusively on Europeans, to an immediate threat, as Mercersburg gained influence in America, Hodge's reaction and leadership of the opposition reflected more than irritation at German intellectual snobbery.

Originally, Hodge simply echoed a familiar cry. His review of Schaff's *Anglogermanismus* called the German speculative reasoning "worthless," and he lamented that so many gifted German writers ignored practical questions of real worth and, instead, wasted their time "earning immortality by efforts to discover what is non-existent and to do what is impossible."[44] While the review is not entirely hostile, Hodge does refute Schaff's main thesis, arguing that in his opinion German speculative theology had not advanced the cause of the Christian religion, but rather inhibited it.

After Nevin published *The Mystical Presence* (1846), Hodge's admonitions developed into deeper criticism. *The Mystical Presence* confirmed for Hodge how dependent Nevin was on German idealism. As a result, Hodge called Nevin a disciple of Schleiermacher, a title sure to arouse evangelical ire.

While there was certainly substance to Hodge's observation, it was odd that he failed to weight more heavily Nevin's even greater and more immediate indebtedness to the German mediating theologian Carl Ullmann, whose essay "The Distinctive Character of Christianity" prefaced the book, and whose work Nevin believed corrected the imbalance within Schleiermacher.[45] More importantly, *The Mystical Presence* began an exchange between Hodge and Nevin that represented an early, first literary example of the best of religious, historical debate in nineteenth-century America.[46]

As a result of the controversy, Mercersburg encouraged and in this case provoked a host of evangelicals to study history, as history was becoming the new filter of epistemology; and Hodge was no exception. Of course, this is to point out that the study of history in America was

---

43. Hodge, "Schaf's Protestantism," review of *Principle of Protestantism*, 626.

44. Hodge, review of *Der Anglogermanismus*, 482–83.

45. Ullmann, "Distinctive Character of Christianity."

46. For a discussion of this debate see my, "Real Presence or Real Absence? The Spoils of War in Nineteenth-Century American Eucharistic Controversy."

fledgling, and the quality of historical facts and argumentation reflected that immaturity. Still, Hodge was forced to face Nevin in debate over Princeton's theory of the development of Reformed doctrine.

The literary debate began in earnest in 1848 with Hodge's review of *The Mystical Presence*. The tenor of Hodge's attack startled the Mercersburg professors because they had considered Hodge sympathetic in their cause against revivalism. They had no inkling how deeply disturbed Hodge was over Mercersburg's support of German idealism and the historical theories coming out of Germany.

Hodge began his review by identifying Princeton as the institution entrusted with the job of assessing the true historical record in opposition to the one proposed by speculative theology. Furthermore, Hodge confirmed Princeton's conclusion that Mercersburg be placed among the German idealists most associated with rationalism, pantheism, and confused notions of historical development.

In his review, Hodge maintained that Nevin's philosophical foundation depended on the imbalanced theories of Leibniz, whose studies in monism sought to replace classical dualism. For Hodge, monism's failures read like Shelley's novel, where a Frankenstein's monster, whose unmatched body parts and fused and artificial life mocked itself even as it animated its own wretched and unholy existence. Like the monster, the monistic systems were not made by God, but by man's own devilry.

Said Hodge, so mocks the system of Leibniz, as if the chasm between body and soul, at his command, could be sown closed; as if the horrible fusion of the real substances of body and soul could ultimately ignore their eternal and irreconcilable differences. Hodge insisted that only real entities constitute genus or species. Identity can only be established as "real substances" act on discrete particulars. That which constitutes species or genus is a real substance. Thus, life is not an essence. Rather, "life" is a general term for the sum of living things. In fact, what "lives" is life. Life is a predicable. For there to be life, something must live! In effect, in strictest condemnation of the language of German idealism, life is not a thing by itself.[47]

Hodge believed he knew what the practical religious implications of idealism were, especially as they had surfaced in the Mercersburg camp: Nevin and Schaff had irresponsibly confused the difference

47. Hodge, "Nature of Man," 111–35.

between substance and essence and allowed their mingling. Thus their confusion of Christ's two natures marred the distinction between his human nature and his divine nature. Furthermore, as Mercersburg weighed itself on the side of Christ's human nature, they left undistinguished the person of Christ and the person of the believer. In other words, they confused themselves with Christ. The result was the sin of vanity and pride and, worse, the heresy of pantheism: a monstrosity that divinizes fallen humanity.

Hodge was vociferous in his conclusion that such a heresy will surely jeopardize the future of the church. Tragically, lamented Hodge, this heresy appeared at a time in America when the Reformation's re-pristination of the original church in Protestantism had issued in such wonderful success in interdenominational cooperation. In America, argued Hodge, true piety and real unity had advanced the cause of Christendom and were winning the war against the monarchistic and tyrannical schemes of the Italian papacy. Sadly, he concluded, Mercersburg would reverse this direction.

Hodge believed that such practical consequences, especially as they led to sympathy for Roman Catholicism and an emphasis on the visible church, betrayed the materialism in Hegelian thinking. Said Hodge, no wonder Mercersburg would rail against the true and more ancient understanding of the church as the invisible communion of the saints, "the body of those who are united to Christ by the indwelling of his spirit."[48] Said Hodge, the church is no visible hierarchy, and she has no leader but Christ. Christ, alone, invisibly rules, through the Holy Spirit.

As a modern, theological scientist Hodge was product enough of his age to offer metaphysical "proofs" for his claims, which he applied according to the inductive method of the day. These proofs form a rough outline of his theology, and they clearly indicate Hodge's philosophical preference for "realistic dualism." In outline form, Hodge's argument remains, to this day, a significant source of contemporary evangelical theology.[49] In fairness to Hodge, it must be observed that

---

48. Hodge, "Idea of the Church," 249–52.

49. "Evangelical" is used here in the modern sense of the term, and designates a broad grouping of churches coming into prominence after the Civil War. They were solidified by revival styles of worship, they tended to be nonconfessional in identity (often preferring covenants or a conservative or literal interpretation of the Bible), and they usually emphasized personal piety. Typically they shared a zeal for individual

Nevin summarized his adversary's outline in a terse and overly simple manner. Yet in spite of the absence of nuance, the outline is accurately represented. (Keep in mind that Hodge's outline appears reactionary, as Hodge understood himself in opposition to Nevin and thus, countering Nevin's arguments.)

First is the thesis that salvation history is revelational and static. It does not evolve, nor does it unfold in a series of stages. Said Hodge, the idealistic concept of historic evolution is characteristic of Newman's approach, which is simply a defense of the papacy. In fact, the apostolic church of Christ, originally perfect and unblemished, was somehow shanghaied and quickly compromised by certain corrupt leaders in Rome. That began the centuries-old apostasy where church unity, previously identified in the "indwelling" of God's Spirit with its members, was suddenly and wrongly identified in the corrupt episcopate.

Hodge's second thesis is that, as with the true church, which is heaven-sent and perfect, so also is doctrine heaven-sent, existing supernaturally where it can be found on the pages of the Bible. Doctrine comes to full expression and maturity in the heart of the individual Christian believer, as the believer realizes a personal maturity in its understanding. This is in direct contrast to the idealistic view that doctrine itself is evolving, and that doctrine matures in historical Christian experience.

Third is the thesis that the Reformation represents the restoration of Christian practice and teaching. The Middle Ages were a great apostasy and blight upon history, as dark as the forces they served.

Last is the thesis that the benefits and insights of Christianity, indeed of faith itself, come to the individual solely from Christ through the influence of the Holy Spirit, unmediated and direct. The church is not essential for imparting faith, nor is it the sole repository of the grace that saves.

---

conversion and, often, participated in loose alliances with similar church groups engaged in proselytizing, foreign missions, and humanitarian ventures. Surely it was the cooperative ventures of the nineteenth century, along with the popularity of a "revival" style worship that helped launch these churches into prominence. The evolution of the word "evangelical" is an interesting one for our time. A description of the changes in the meaning of "evangelical" can be found in my "Saving Evangelical Catholicism for Today," 11–20. These Protestants would become the core of the Christian right of contemporary American religion.

Clearly Hodge reflects the perspective in which individual insight and decision making are paramount, and where that individual decision making is most crucial is in accepting the offering made by Christ at Calvary. Thus he represents the significant theological voice of authority validating the concept that what is really important is the believer's personal relationship with Jesus Christ because in that relationship is vouchsafed for the believer the benefits of the atonement!

In summary, Hodge suggests that Mercersburg's theological confusion was matched by their historical confusion. Their German idealistic philosophy, their softness on Rome, and their preoccupation with the sacraments made them lose sight of what created the church's original unity and what sustains it today. So, at the heart of the controversy was the debate over the church's past, especially the Reformation, and what constituted authentic Reformed ecclesiology and sacramental tradition. Hodge felt confident in his understanding of the past, and he pressed the challenge to debate with Mercersburg on the subject of Reformed church history. Mercersburg wasted no time in taking up the gauntlet.

The Counterattack

Schaff was quick to reply to Hodge's attack, and he first addressed his comments to the German-speaking community by means of an article in *Der Deutsche Kirchenfreund*, "Princeton und Mercersburg." Schaff allowed that Hodge and Alexander must be reckoned with, since their familiarity with the new German learning came from direct study while traveling there. Still, Schaff's complaint was that they had no sympathy with German philosophy, nor did they desire to benefit from its insights. Rather, they took from German research only the things that appealed to them, points where German theological science "does not conflict with their traditional orthodoxy." Schaff was indignant that Princeton would turn America against German philosophy "although they naively confess they don't understand it."[50]

In "Princeton und Mercersburg," Schaff identified himself as a leader, with Nevin, in the controversial Mercersburg movement, and the "instigator" of the controversy with the publication of *The Principle of Protestantism*. He expressed surprise that Hodge's reaction was

---

50. "Princeton und Mercersburg," 154–55. Translation mine: *obwhol sie hier und da schon das naive Gestandniss abgelegt haben, das sie davon eigentlich nichts verstehen.*

delayed, but he recognized that all that Hodge disliked about *The Mystical Presence* applied equally to *The Principle of Protestantism*, since they occupied the same historical and theological ground.

Schaff wrote in the *Kirchenfreund* that he was driven by Hodge to declare his allegiance and stand with Nevin and the Mercersburg theology, dissolving whatever friendly relations had previously existed with Princeton, if need be. He concluded his declaration saying, the time had come to pick up the "weapons of self-defense."

The warlike language was only just beginning. Nevin's subsequent response to Hodge's review was titled "Antichrist: Or the Spirit of Sect and Schism," and it intensified the atmosphere of open conflict, declaring an assault on the "Antichrist." Nevin wasn't going so far as to call Hodge the Antichrist, but he was placing Princeton among those leaders and movements who most threatened the "cause of Christ" in America, identifying them with the Antichrist.

Hodge's review convinced Mercersburg that Hodge was the spokesman for the "modern Puritan" position occupied by a collegial body of Protestant denominations loosely aligned, who recognized each other's right to exist. Nevin's initial response to the unofficial representative of that association was a declaration of war on all those sympathetic to his "unchurchly" tendencies. The effect was to initiate

> . . . a regular assault upon the sect system, as being in full antagonism to the true idea of the Church, and such a heresy as draws after it virtually in the end a Gnostic denial of the proper mystery of the Incarnation itself.[51]

Of course, Nevin was defensive about Hodge's associating him with Hegel and Schleiermacher, again appealing to the record to demonstrate his standing with the mediating school. But the most telling criticism made by Nevin of Hodge was that Hodge was so weak a student of history that he must depend on Nevin to make his case. What is clear from the debate is that Hodge was relying on what had been

---

51. This quotation appeared in a letter written by Nevin to the Reverend Dr. Harbaugh in 1872. Although a second-generation Mercersburg leader, Henry Harbaugh became almost as influential as Schaff and Nevin. His work in hymnody provides a treasured legacy among German Reformed congregations. The letter was recovered from the personal papers of the Reverend Amos Seldomridge, and was published in *Catholic and Reformed: Selected Writings by John W. Nevin*. The quote appears on page 1 of the letter.

the common understanding of the development of Reformed doctrine, simply repudiating what Nevin said he found in the doctrines themselves. That is, for whatever reason, Hodge was not disposed to hang his criticism of Nevin on original research.

Nevin declared that at the crux of the debate was the issue of the incarnation, and how God's life entered the world's life. Hodge believed that his understanding of the infusion of spiritual life to the individual by means of the Holy Spirit derived from the ancient Reformed sources. Nevin lambasted that position, maintaining that Hodge simply assumed that the theology of Princeton and the "modern Puritan" theology mirrored that of Calvin and the Reformers.

Nevin had been busy studying the original sources, seeking to unearth the architecture of Reformation doctrine. His research uncovered a sacramental position in Calvin that must have surprised and delighted him, and he used that position as a corrective to what he perceived was a modern, Protestant imbalance in the doctrine of the Holy Supper.

Nevin revealed that Calvin placed great emphasis on sacramental grace, more than was commonly thought. Nevin incorporated this information into his argument about the way God dispenses God's life to the church. He concluded that a churchly theology that places less emphasis on the role of the individual and more emphasis on corporate responsibility would correct the modern sectarian tendency. Said Nevin (with Schaff in full agreement), emphasizing individual experience encourages a direct appeal to individual authority: the moment of conception in the life of a sect.

Mercersburg's recovery of the ancient doctrinal sources was a deliberate attempt to educate Americans about the relative immaturity of contemporary Protestant practice. In place of this practice, Nevin and Schaff produced a historically defended view whereby a sacramental church would abandon current Eucharistic and baptismal attitudes; where, in their view, the sacraments' role was instrumental and auxiliary; and allow the mystery and power of the Supper itself to become central to the life and faith of both church and believer.

Clearly what was behind much of the debate with Hodge was Mercersburg's persistent question about the nature of God's participation in people's lives by means of the sacrament of Holy Communion. Nevin wrote,

> What he [Hodge] is offended with is the conception of *sacramental religion*, as distinguished from a religion of mere individual spirituality. . . . Justification by faith and sacramental grace are, in his view, incompatible conceptions.[52]

What Hodge failed to see, argued Mercersburg, was that thanks to German historical science, the ancient doctrines provided the answer and the corrective to the current imbalanced exclusion of sacramental grace from American Protestant theology. Nevin was able to use his historical research to gain an advantage over Hodge. Hodge was left in the predicament of defending his sacramental position without confidence that the traditional sources supported that position.

Having no choice but to accede to Nevin the historical ground, Hodge was left to argue that, effectively, the Reformed doctrines of the sixteenth century reflect the adjustment of Reformed thinking as it encountered often hostile views within the various Protestant camps. He concluded that in most cases, the rough doctrines agreed to by the Reformers were attempts at compromise with Lutherans, thus they hardly reflect the "true source" of Reformed practice and piety.

Nevin found Hodge's view cowardly; and Hodge's appeal to the Consensus Tigurinus, a document never held authoritative for the Reformed, to discredit Calvin, seemed especially revealing of the weakness of his argument. Indeed, Nevin ridiculed Hodge for repeating the same mistake that Westphal had made hundreds of years earlier. Westphal used the Consensus to depict Calvin as a deeply sacramental Lutheran who felt obligated to placate the belligerent Swiss, for whom the Lord's Supper was predominantly a memorial. The oddity, said Nevin, was that Hodge reversed the argument, using the Consensus to pretend that Calvin was a closet Swiss desperately seeking to win over Lutherans.[53]

Ultimately Hodge would argue that Zwingli was the best ancient representative of Reformed orthodoxy and that his theology was closest to the current Reformed position on the matter of sacramental grace. Nevin agreed on the latter point, although Nevin insisted that even Zwingli had a higher view of the sacrament than did the churches unofficially represented by Hodge. In Nevin's view, American sacramental

---

52. Nevin, "Sacramental Religion," 131.
53. Nevin, "Doctrine of the Reformed Church on the Lord's Supper," 487.

practice was a new phenomenon, born of a sectarian spirit, defended by an individualistic rationale, and founded upon an antiquated philosophical premise: common-sense realism and its source in traditional dualism. It had compromised itself with a general perspective that recoiled at the idea of union with the human Christ and, with it, the idea that a mingling of divine and human flesh is necessary for corporeal life to be infused with spiritual life.

Grim Resolution

Hodge's attack convinced Mercersburg that American evangelicals were hostile to the Mercersburg theology. That a controversy was seething from the very beginning seems clear from the advantage of hindsight. Realism and idealism proposed vastly different views of reality. Mercersburg was just as aggressive in denying realism a place in American orthodoxy as evangelicals were in denying German idealism a place. In some ways, Mercersburg was the more uncompromising.

Nevin considered common-sense realism counterspiritual. His view was that realism's shyness about the fact of supernatural existence shut it out from any experience of true mystery and therefore of the divine, and he was quick to blame Locke and Bacon for suggesting the antireligious philosophy. Said Nevin, in spite of the practical benefits derived from their work, Locke and Bacon failed Christianity by wresting from it its most sacred task: the quest for the Absolute.[54]

In revealing this ultimate failure, Nevin and Schaff believed they exposed the core of realists' thinking and the source of their error. Mercersburg contended that realists seek to study the world from "pure objectivity," with Locke depicting the world on a *tabula rasa*, whereby all practical objects of experience neatly corresponded with our idea of them. But, concluded Mercersburg, such philosophical tidiness could not do justice to the infinite, which required full participation in the life of nature and reason.

Philosophically Nevin followed Rauch, confessing the limits of German idealism, as much as he recognized the shortcomings of common-sense realism. The fusion he proposed in his introduction to Schaff's *Principle of Protestantism* echoed the evangelical approach of the first American representative of German mediating thought. Here

54. Nevin, "Human Freedom," 34–35.

he took his stand, pressing the case of the supernatural over against the "merely real."[55] Nevin conceded there were excessive elements in all philosophies, but he believed the excesses of German idealism could be corrected by bending its will to serve the evangelical faith. In contrast, Nevin resolved that the excesses of common-sense realism nullified it as a "true philosophy." It could not do justice to a world that it could not verify.

For Mercersburg, giving such lofty respect to instrumental reasoning found in common-sense realism opened the floodgates to the excesses that naturally followed: rationalism and skepticism. Hence Nevin pronounced the verdict in the case of common-sense realism, judging it to be a bogus philosophy.

Nevin especially believed that realism could not address rationalism because realism had no power to apprehend the immanent forces that underlie reality. In effect, realism could not appreciate the "spiritual" aspect of life. Said Nevin, in its specious abstraction of life and in the sterile objectivity of its empirical method, it treated life as an anatomically dissected, "dead subject" rather than as a "living force." Unconcerned with the organic relatedness of life, and how that inward unity directs the development of history, realism was unable to appreciate the dynamic that made history a living thing. The realists, with their rationalistic bent, ignored this and treated history as a succession of ideas or doctrines. Together, Mercersburg concluded that it would never do to pretend that human experience could be removed from the movement of history.

> We are shut up thus to the idea of historical development . . . Growth implies unity in the midst of change. That is precisely what we are to understand by historical development.[56]

Nevin observed that the American tendency to understand history as a progression of ideas satisfied the status quo teaching of a church whose visible quality must be held apart from its invisible quality. Consistent with common-sense religion's rationale, the qualities corresponded to discrete and separate entities. That led to the mistaken belief that there really was a "visible church," and that there really was an "invisible church." The visible church was the gathered membership.

---

55. Nevin, "Introduction to Schaff's *Principle of Protestantism*," 7.
56. Nevin, "Early Christianity" 32–33.

The invisible church (the "true church") was the fellowship of those bound together by the Holy Spirit.

For Mercersburg, common-sense religion's thinking on this issue became even cloudier because as the binding was inward and invisible, it became impossible to tell who was and who was not in the invisible Church. Nevin's caricature of this was of a phantom church: a disembodied entity.

Mercersburg found the divisive description of the church as both visible and invisible to be subjective and individualistic, and Nevin believed it led to the burgeoning American notion of the church as "resting upon its members." In contrast, Mercersburg argued that the members rest upon the church, and while they would occasionally speak of the visible and invisible church themselves, they understood the terms as heuristic descriptions and not ontological realities.

More often, Mercersburg spoke of the inward or subjective form of the church or, in contrast, the outward or objective form of the church. In their analysis, Protestantism's dialectical imbalance stressed the inward form. In this, Mercersburg identified a common ailment of American ecclesiology, i.e., that evangelicals considered the invisible fellowship to constitute the only "true" church. The theological implications were obvious, concluded Mercersburg: Ultimately the objective form of the church was ignored.[57]

With time and mounting assaults, Mercersburg's evangelical audience grew suspicious. It seemed to them that Mercersburg was lifting the outward form of the church to Protestant America's attention simply as a devious and unwanted attempt to promote the visible church over the invisible church. That, for many, seemed to be the very intention of "Rome."

In contrast, Mercersburg argued that the church was an objective, historical institution imbued with divine life. To understand this life required an understanding of church history, as researched in a scientific (objective) manner. Sadly however, concluded the Mercersburg

---

57. The extreme use of language in criticizing opponents was characteristic of both sides of the argument. Throughout the corpus, the harshest language is used to dramatize the failure of the opposing side. In truth, neither side "utterly ignored" the visible or invisible qualities of the church, and both sides spoke of this ancient polarity. In American evangelical circles, the prominence of a visible church figured into their stress on piety, church attendance, the role of the pastor, and in a multitude of other ways.

professors, the history of the church that Americans were familiar with was the familiar record of biblical epochs and confessional statements. It contained little mention of the struggles behind the development of doctrines since it assumed that revelation entered into human experience from above. This approach to history kept philosophy at arm's length.

The novelty of German idealism, as practiced by Mercersburg, made history and philosophy codependent. History was the record of philosophic development, and philosophy provided the significance (idea) of that historic record. Because Americans appeared to Mercersburg to be unconcerned about the significance of history, and because American philosophy provided the conditions for understanding but not "understanding itself," Mercersburg concluded that, in fact, Americans deplored philosophy. They certainly did, for the most part, deplore idealist philosophy. But Nevin strains to suggest that Americans had no philosophy at all.

Nevin's argument was that in abrogating responsibility for being history's conscience, Americans had come to prefer a banal appeal to "common sense" over philosophy. This led him to defiantly call American realism no philosophy at all, but a substitute for serious critical thought. He vilified realism as a rubber stamp for traditional concepts.

Again, to Mercersburg, this muzzling of self-reflection led to the dulling of American intellect and spirit, and made Christianity in the United States a faith without a philosophy. Nevin wrote, in what was clearly a statement displaying his romantic zeal, that while "an unphilosophical Christianity may be sufficient to save a multitude of individual souls for heaven . . . it can never conquer the world."[58]

Nevin followed his declaration with this condemnation, that in common-sense realism's emphasis on "outward" consciousness, as produced by a single-mindedness toward practical issues, it did not seek to be profound. Of course, Hodge saw only the pompous and not the profound in idealism. To him, idealism's manufacture of profound thoughts was quixotic, and the ideas that Nevin would have Americans wrestle with were so many windmills. After all, Hodge complained, what is profound is reliable, and what is more reliable than to seek to

---

58. Nevin, "Human Freedom," 40.

"measure all things . . . by the categories of the common abstract understanding, as it stands related to the world of time and sense"?[59]

Nevin believed that this was not only incomplete but also naive. He argued that in Kant or, better, after critical reflection on Kant's conclusions, philosophy came to recognize the categories of abstract understanding as categories of thought, but not of life. He concluded that in Princeton's loyalty to the tradition of Locke, they ran aground, where Hume's doubts left no safe harbor. This "false and helpless" system barricaded itself in the entrenched thinking of evangelicals, among others, and came to dominate "our whole life." It had a natural tendency toward materialism and anarchy, and it deceived itself by pretending that the spiritual and supernatural existed within its own "province," while, in fact, Princeton's system had "no power to reach the spiritual and supernatural." Instead it manufactured an image of scientific rigor by arguing "proofs" for Christian doctrine in the style of Bacon. At its heart, Nevin concluded, it was no true science at all, but a confused common-sense based reasoning that boasted of "experience" in place of a rigorous epistemology.[60]

Nevin summarized his position with regard to realism in a review of Horace Bushnell's *Natural and the Supernatural, as together consisting of one system of God*. Nevin maintained that realism treats the supernatural as a "transient phenomenon": an irregular appearance of the unnatural in the natural, a "theophany only in the Old Testament style." Pushing the metaphor of organic union, Nevin linked the supernatural to a person's natural capacity for faith. The supernatural

> must then be supremely natural, as well as overwhelmingly supernatural; no product of nature plainly, and yet in such harmony with it, that it shall seem to be at the same time its full outbursting glory and necessary perfection.[61]

Nevin came to realize that his position was unpopular and unlikely to gain support among the majority of Americans. In this sense, argued Nevin, the age was at "war" with the gospel. Said Nevin, it ignored the supernatural and embraced rationalism, and he suggested that modern humanism was a symptom of that same misguided rationalism. He

59. Ibid., 42.
60. Ibid.
61. Nevin, "Natural and Supernatural," 176–77.

observed that even the pious attempts of Christian people to inaugurate the "Kingdom of God" by means of social programs was errant, rationalistic, and the reoccurring, heretical return to the "Jewish Messianic error." Here the act of salvation was applied directly to the "natural economy," as if the supernatural economy had no role to play. This idea had the supernatural economy in subjection to the natural economy, while, in fact, the ultimate subjection of the natural economy to the "new" economy of grace was the first principle of Christian faith given to us in the incarnation.

In a fascinating article (given Nevin's earlier social activism), he argued that misguided Christians (as well as Jews) persist in viewing the kingdom of heaven as merely the continuation and fulfillment of the proper and original idea of the world from creation. It is the expectation that what this world was meant to be is seeking daily to actualize itself and bring itself into being. It commends itself to humanists and those who believe that even though the dream of human harmony seems distant and the "kingdom" far away, things can be done today to move the world closer to the dream and its fulfillment. By so doing, by becoming allies with those who share noble ideals and the means to achieve those ideals, the figment is that humanity can bring the world closer to the kingdom of God. Nevin despaired of this logic and wrote:

> Such is the humanitarian evangel, which in one form or another has come to prevail so widely especially in our own time, thrusting itself into the place of the true gospel of our Lord and Savior Jesus Christ.[62]

Again, the danger Nevin saw in this was the growing phenomenon of American humanism and the way he believed it compromised the supernatural foundation of Christianity. For Mercersburg, it was the too-close identification of the exclusive (if seemingly well-meaning) interests of humanity with those of the gospel. The humanitarian dream or goal was a wolf in sheep's clothing and, so, a clever heresy, because it seemed to conform to the most basic Christian interests: the redemption of fallen humanity. But the flawed messianic dream rested upon the natural, and so it made the kingdom of grace to rest on humanity and thus suggested that the kingdom's fulfillment was simply the final chapter in nature's orderly process.

62. Nevin, "Jesus and the Resurrection," 183.

The mistaken humanistic conclusion, argued Nevin, was that human science and art were subject to human control. In contrast, he insisted, the process of redemption was not at all natural, but supernatural and so in God's control. Society was in grave danger of thinking that material interests were identical to spiritual interests, that profit and success were signs of godliness, and that political and commercial achievements were the triumphs of a Christian state. Warned Nevin, the cause of the ambitious and practical cannot be confused with the intangible "hope" and "battle" for individual rights—and freedom cannot become synonymous with heaven's plan of salvation. Nevin concluded:

> The kingdom of heaven is no mere continuation or carrying forward of the order of this life, whether physical or ethical; it is constitutionally different from this; and is to be reached and possessed only as the whole system of things seen and temporal is superseded at last, through death and resurrection, by things unseen and eternal.[63]

Mercersburg contented that realist-informed theology literally stunted the growth of the kingdom of God by making its appearance in the natural world mechanical and artificial. The accusation was made in a historical analysis of how revelation entered the world of sense. Mercersburg's speculative, historical analysis sought to explain the process that led to the present crisis. They argued that the Reformers of the sixteenth century rejected the papacy as the source of divine revelation and replaced an infallible pope with an infallible book. The effect of the Reformation was that the Bible alone, by means of the Spirit, would convey God's words to the world. In time, said Mercersburg, the Bible itself was perceived as a divine object in the world. Thus a form of "bibliolatry" became widespread among Protestants. The eventual effect of this "bibliolatry" made the Bible simply a "proof text" for favorite Protestant dogmas. With too much emphasis on the texts themselves (as literal word rather than "living word"), the seeds of rationalistic doubt were planted; a doubt that would contribute to Christianity's swing away from the ancient mystical foundation of faith and towards a humanistic perspective.

Mercersburg's analysis recognized both the contribution and excesses of biblical criticism. They argued that in reaction to the exclusion

63. Ibid., 184.

of the "human" and "literary" quality of Scripture, a form of rationalistic doubt became prevalent. It too was taken to the extreme, and Mercersburg believed that the two opposing positions were damagingly entrenched in the American experience.

Oddly enough, the Protestant, evangelical position copied the Roman Catholic doctrine of verbal inspiration. The theory held that the Holy Spirit inspired, for example, the apostles, who were likely illiterate men yet by the Spirit's power were able to transcribe God's own words. Mercersburg argued that the obvious mechanical quality of this position revealed its dualistic influence, in that the supernatural breaks into the natural by way of the miraculous.

In contrast, Mercersburg insisted that the authority of the canon came from the living presence of Christ, which the text contained. As much as the supernatural was present in the natural, the living Christ was present in the Bible.

Mercersburg concluded that only in appeal to the person of Christ was correct interpretation of Scripture possible. Since faith comes not from Scripture but from Christ, so, also, faith must take its starting point from Christ and not from the Bible. Biblical faith, then, said Mercersburg, is not faith in the Bible's ability to be supported by outward evidence. It is not an issue of scientific credibility or the Bible's reasonability or its factual consistency. Biblical faith is the recognition that what is supernaturally objective in the person of Christ as encountered by the individual is substantiated in the outward and physical presentation of the faith as contained in Scripture. In other words, it is not the Bible that commends us to Christ. It is Christ who commends us to Scripture.

As criticism to their system mounted, Mercersburg began to identify a common link in American anti-idealist thinking. In review of American philosophical history, Mercersburg maintained that common sense and practical reasoning necessarily divided experience according to the elevated place it gave to individual experience. Theologically this led to a general identification of the supernatural quality of the gospel and the church, with subjective systems, each claiming "divine authority."

In contrast, Mercersburg required philosophers to seek unifying themes, voluntarily giving up the positions that might further their particular ends and sacrificing them for the greater good, which would naturally be recognition of a sublime sacramental unity above all else. Such a theme made participation in the supernatural economy the only legitimate authentication of divine approval. Mercersburg concluded that their analysis revealed that as the tendency increased for Protestants throughout America to reject the sacraments as "divine acts . . . working towards salvation," division and disaffection followed.[64]

Mercersburg believed that the widespread minimizing of the importance of the sacraments as "divine acts" among American denominations had varying levels of impact depending on the denomination. While it was a fundamental characteristic among Baptists, it had worked its way into the Lutheran, Reformed, Methodist, Presbyterian, and Congregational churches. Episcopalians, by nature more used to viewing the sacraments as supernatural events, were divided on the issue. However, many of their "lower" churches, churches that downplayed the importance of the liturgy and ecclesiastical tradition, shared the view with other evangelicals that the sacraments were merely symbols or signs.

That so many denominations shared this view led Mercersburg to conclude that its source was a common one and, likewise, that behind the growing sectarian tendency was a common error. The error was stripping the supernatural of its power and presence within the sphere of common human experience, and regulating it to the uncommon and, in Mercersburg's view, mythic sphere of an unnatural world. The concept they employed to describe the unwholesome severance of supernatural experience, a division that robbed people of the richest half of the fullness of human experience, was of a "false dualism."

Repairing the rift meant providing the glue that held God's world and humanity's world together. That "glue" could not be all spirit, nor could it be all matter. It needed to be both, sharing the essence of each. It could not be abstract either, as in Kant's categories. It had to share life and being with the things it achieved unity with, and so was a

---

64. This theme is undercurrent in Schaff's, *Principle of Protestantism*. The ideal of enlightened thinking that would give up its own position for the more comprehensive vision is evident in Nevin's bold political tract, "Party Spirit," where he makes his argument against political pluralism. The sacramental and churchly appeal is made in his "Pseudo-Protestantism."

"hypostatic union." That "glue," offered by Mercersburg, taking their lead from the meditating school, was the person of Christ.[65]

The criticism that arose in evangelical protest of this view accused Mercersburg of mingling Christ's essence with the essence of the believer and so deifying the believer. Mercersburg responded that the unity we share with the divinity is accomplished by union with Christ, where by the individual's faith and by the Spirit's power, the "humanity" of Christ is joined to the believer's soul. This allowed full participation in Christ's divinity (and humanity) with no hint of a pantheistic identification of humanity with God.

Mercersburg was not shy about insisting that union with God was essential. The role of the Holy Spirit was thus reversed in Mercersburg's system. Mercersburg accused evangelicals of using the Holy Spirit to guard Christ's transcendence. In this "pernicious" system, as mediator, it was the Spirit who communicated with the world of men and women, but in a mechanical way that prevented the real mingling of personalities. Mercersburg wanted to restore a traditional concept of the Spirit as the source of real union: the divine person who closes, rather than maintains, the gap between heaven and earth.

As evangelical philosophy and religion came to represent the conscience of conservative America, Mercersburg believed the gap between heaven and earth was widening. While revivals stirred people to religious ecstasy, the heightened spirituality's effect was of individual justification. Such emphasis on the individual over the community fostered a divisive and self-serving pluralism in American politics. That, along with a concomitant fixation with material success as the source of personal worth, fueled the growing exploitation of nature and the tendency to idolize technology, to the detriment of the arts. Nevin wrote:

> All we need to protest against in this case, is the insanity of making nature, in its own sphere, the end of all knowledge; the madness of imagining, that the moral interests can ever be subordinated safely to material interests; the wild hallucination of dreaming, that the great battle and work of life for man is to be accomplished by physics and mechanics, by insight simply into the laws of nature and mastery of its powers, by chemistry, geology, mineralogy, metallurgy, and other such studies, by

---

65. For more on this subject, see Schaff's *Christ and Christianity* and Nevin's "Christianity and Humanity."

polytechnic ingenuity and skill applied in all manner of ways to business and trade. There is a higher view than all this, in which the study of nature becomes itself the study of mind, and the material meets us everywhere as the sacrament of the spiritual and divine.[66]

Mercersburg's advice, couched in their philosophical idiom, was so foreign to their American antagonists that it fell on deaf ears. After all, Princeton had long believed that life was not being. Therefore, they could not conceive of measuring the quality of the nation's "spirit" in the terms used by Mercersburg. The issue of pluralism, if considered at all, would need to be critiqued in terms of pluralism's so-called moral success or failure (as measured by the canon of Scripture).

For example, if the affairs of state went well, and a form of pluralism was apparent, well, what of it? You see, practical and moral success were at the heart of it, and the Holy Spirit's mark would be duly identified in that simple quality of success, even as it is today so marked by the "Religious Right." In contrast, for Mercersburg, the idea of sacrifice for the greater good, as a moral disposition superior to one of self-advancement, no matter the outcome, was the way one embraced "being" and demonstrated how the divine was moving the world, developmentally, in an upward manner. It also revealed the way that God was at work in the world. Yet, for Mercersburg, seeing God in the world required that Christ be at the center of the state's consciousness.[67]

Given Mercersburg's unique christocentrism, it is not surprising that when the evangelicals at Princeton refined their attack on Mercersburg, it centered on what Princeton believed was Mercersburg's

66. Nevin, "Commencement Address," 40. Contrast this remarkable nineteenth-century prophecy with the following quotation from John Kenneth Galbraith's *The Age of Uncertainty*. Galbraith is describing the modern "technostructure," which, in their "organizational competence," are all alike. Galbraith wrote, "These men of the technostructure are the new and universal priesthood. Their religion is business success; their test of virtue is growth and profit. Their bible is the computer printout; their communion bench is the committee room. The sales force carries their message to the world, and a message is what it is often called. Alcohol is under interdict as an intoxicant but allowed as an adjunct of communion and as an instrument of friendly persuasion. Recreation is for regeneration of the business spirit, for a widened range of business contacts. Sex is for better sleep. The Jesuits of this austere faith are the graduates of the Harvard Business School" (271).

67. Ironically, Mercersburg and evangelicals shared the same goal. However, the contest was how to get there!

confusion of the person of Christ. Mercersburg's emphasis of Christ's humanity as the key to organic union raised a host of objections, most of which have been mentioned.

Still, Mercersburg was keen to delineate their "orthodoxy," hoping that the clear articulation of their position might endear them to well-meaning Christians. At the crux of their explanation was a "modern," German-conceived psychology, obviously suspect in America. The question Nevin was asking, simply put, was, what is personality if not the unity of consciousness?

Satisfying this, ipso facto, Mercersburg could assume that Christ's personality had to unite or mediate his divinity and his humanity. The absolute reality of this unity, as organically wedded to natural life, was fundamental to an Athanasian understanding of faith.

For Mercersburg, the characteristic weakness of Princeton's position was the way it erred in the direction of the doctrine of Nestorius. For them, deism and realistic dualism shared this unnatural abstraction. God's transcendence should never be understood in tension with God's immanence. Rather, the deistic and Calvinistic views emphasized God's distinction from nature. Said Nevin, the result was poor theological fare. In this stiff view, God is the great architect, the master designer of the mechanism of nature. Creation's *telos* proceeded from God's eternal decrees, which break into creation from the mind of God in an utterly artificial ("mechanical") way.

Mercersburg faulted Princeton's weak historical understanding for depriving heaven of a living dynamic. Of course, observed Mercersburg, the mechanical view carries over into the natural sphere as well. The complex historical dialectic that demonstrated that a "process" was underway in life suggested, in Princeton's depiction of revelation, that revelation was merely the act of the divine encountering receptive individuals and so enlightening them. Thus it missed the unfolding of revelation in real, human life.

For example, argued Mercersburg, in the "modern Puritan" outlook (they were thinking specifically of Hodge and Princeton—but also generally of the common-sense approach of American Protestant religion), Adam's sin is juridically and arbitrarily imputed to Adam and his children, according to "God's sovereign pleasure." The drama of life becomes the allegoric record of the pilgrims' progress, as Adam's children are "placed on the same theatre . . . for moral trial." Meanwhile, justification is dispensed with equal indifference, to the ones fortunate enough to be "elect."[68]

What Mercersburg pointed out, in this unkind depiction of common-sense religion's doctrine of the atonement, is that the incarnation is given less emphasis than the atonement. Nevin continued his revealing criticism of common-sense religion, with language not meant to leave the reader unmoved: "The incarnation is an expedient, contrived to solve the problem of the atonement, and must be carefully held aloof from the whole process of the world's history under any other view, lest it should lose this 'ex machina' character."[69] Herein also, revealed Nevin, grew the roots of the Jewish messianic heresy, as the dispensation which issues from the mind of God makes the Old Testament saints of equal standing in relationship with God as the New Testament saints. Nevin wrote: "The person of Christ itself, as such, forms not the specific revelation of the gospel, but simply his word and work as instrumentally disclosed through its agency."[70]

The problem with this view, observed Mercersburg, is that the benefits of Christ's words and work don't derive so much from his actual life in the world or from who he is, but from his "theophanic form, in which it was thought good that the Word should at this time appear." As much as the life of Christ is a result of the operation of the mind of God, so the benefits of Christ's sacrifice are imputed to the believer by means of "divine thought." The ongoing relationship of Christ with the world, as Christ remains "seated at God's right hand," is by means of the Spirit, with Christ being present only by proxy. Stated succinctly, Mercersburg believed that the Old School Presbyterians at Princeton sublimated nature in grace, making the invisible world of spirit philosophically subservient to the visible world of sense experience.[71]

Once again, Mercersburg was convinced that with every question raised by the practitioners of common-sense religion against the speculative theology, they had supplied the right answer, and that behind every question, in a philosophical sense, American evangelicals were demonstrating their growing detachment from the ancient catholic,

---

68. Nevin, "Sacramental," 136.
69. Ibid.
70. Ibid.
71. Ibid.

supernatural body brought into the world by Christ. Bolstered by a superior understanding of the ancient texts and by their enthusiasm for German speculative science, Mercersburg was unwilling to cower before the numerical superiority and growing success of American evangelicals. Even as support within the German Reformed Church eroded, and as Nevin and Schaff went their separate ways, Mercersburg's disciples, men such as Henry Harbaugh, E. V. Gerhart and T. Appel, promoted "Mercersburg theology."

In the end, speculative theology remained controversial. Although both Mercersburg and the host of American evangelicals believed rationalism to be a threat, they differed vehemently as to the solution. When Mercersburg concluded that common-sense realism only contributed to the modern-day tendency to exclude God from the ongoing life of the world and to the resulting eclipse of the supernatural from spiritual life, where nature is sublimated in grace, a wedge was driven between the parties. Philosophically, the cause of the rift was Mercersburg's embrace of speculative theology, which sought to reunite the worlds of sense and spirit. Practically, it was the implications of that philosophical and theological embrace.

An example of this includes Mercersburg's appreciation for Roman Catholic tradition, a tradition very comfortable with the experience of the supernatural in the natural. Another example was their critique of "new measures" revivalism, a movement that emphasized a personal encounter with the divine rather than a shared, communal experience dependent on a set, apostolic heritage. Another was the emphasis of the sacraments, where the supernatural inhabited and restored fallen creation in the mystery of the Eucharist.

As controversialists, Mercersburg appeared ever on the defensive, and that rarely bodes well for one's posterity. Nevin virtually began his career at odds with the popular Jacksonian democratic movement, and he equated America's divisive "party spirit" with the Reformation, no doubt antagonizing many of his Protestant readers. In the same tone, he criticized American individualism and "nativism." However, these disputes never developed into full-blown controversy. Headline-making controversy (outside of his abolitionist period) had to wait until Nevin sought the reintroduction of the Heidelberg Catechism for use by the denomination.

Nevin began his work on the Catechism with a series of essays. Few of his readers contested his conclusion that the Catechism was a Calvinistic confession, but several were aghast at his notion that Calvin believed in the real presence of Christ in the Eucharist. (Interestingly, these views had been touched upon by Rauch in an earlier article.[72]) In essence, the ongoing controversy was the result of Nevin's insistence (ultimately with Schaff concurring) that the Catechism was in full sympathy with Catholic tradition.

Nevin's work on the Catechism highlighted Calvin's theology, and here, again, Mercersburg found itself steeped in controversy over the correct interpretation of Calvin. Not that Mercersburg was shy about departing from Calvin at several junctures, but Mercersburg was bold to describe American Reformed Protestant's departure from Calvin, even when they believed themselves to be faithful to the beloved Reformer.

As mentioned above, Mercersburg's controversial stand was strengthened by their familiarity with the ancient texts. Naturally, their critics questioned the way they read those texts, and so Mercersburg found itself in another controversy, this time over history. As previously stated, Mercersburg fundamentally accepted the methodology of German, speculative theology. This controversy was heated and contentious. It effectively began with Schaff's publication of *The Principle of Protestantism* in 1845.

Of course, Schaff's methodology reflected the novel, German approach to history forged by Hegel. But just as important for Mercersburg's detractors, it debunked the idea of a pristine Christianity as recovered with the Reformation, since history is developmental and evolves over time. Things do not typically spring-up without a source. So, naturally, Mercersburg acknowledged Roman Catholicism as the historical source of Protestantism.

The Principle of Protestantism appeared early in Schaff's career. Indeed, it was an expansion of his inaugural address delivered in Reading, Pennsylvania, on October 25th, 1844. It immediately angered Joseph Berg, whose previous address was, in substance, a case for the Reformation as the recovery of original Christianity.

While Berg continued to be one of Mercersburg's most outspoken critics, Schaff and Nevin were only intensifying a controversy that had

---

72. Rauch, "German Characteristics."

begun the year before, with the publication of Nevin's tract called *The Anxious Bench*. For many, that little tract marked Nevin's departure from "modern Puritanism" and set off the most sensational of the many controversial issues of the Mercersburg era, namely the "church question."

The question of the church found Mercersburg sparring with some of the best Christian minds of the century: Hodge, Brownson, Bushnell, Dorner, and Wilberforce. In a certain sense, it might be argued that Mercersburg's position here was centrist, that is, standing more or less in the middle of the European and American nineteenth-century church debate, not siding entirely with the findings of the Oxford movement or the German royalists, but horrifying many in their own denomination by lauding the many virtues of Roman Catholicism. Practically speaking, as much as any other controversy, the church question, with Mercersburg's sacramental stand, led to the harshest criticism they would receive. When the provisional liturgy, so influenced by the Mercersburg professors, finally appeared late in 1857 to a lukewarm reception, it was clear that both Schaff and Nevin were growing weary of their struggles.

Even so, a decade later, Nevin would conclude his career as controversialist battling with one of Germany's leading divines, Isaac Dorner. Once again, some of the initiating forces sparking the controversy were political in nature. Nevin had assumed that Dorner was in agreement with the Mercersburg theology, but antagonists within the domination personally asked for Dorner's support against Mercersburg. Theologically, Dorner and Nevin shared very similar positions and rarely disagreed. Naturally, Nevin was aghast that Dorner would side with his opponents within the German Reformed Church. He argued bitterly that their disagreements were minor compared to Dorner's recorded rejection of the views of Nevin's opponents—the very agents (along with their "Puritanistic system") who had conspired to set Dorner against him. In the end, Nevin plunged deeply into this last, major controversy, this time over Christology, and so Nevin ended his career very much as he began it, in lucid and brilliant, if contentious, controversy.

Conclusion

IN 1862 THE AREA AROUND MERCERSBURG WAS RAIDED BY CONFEDERATE troops. The fierce warfare forced the closing of the seminary in 1863. Schaff found a teaching position at Andover. Nevin gave up most of his denominational responsibilities, and later became president of Franklin and Marshall College.[1]

The older, Calvinistic theology was losing its majority grip on American religion. The country was being pulled in two different directions. "Liberal religion," as marshaled by Universalism,[2] saw tremendous growth during the middle part of the nineteenth century, and while the war marked the slowing of Unitarian growth, "rationalism," as Mercersburg termed it, became the dominant feature of American theology. Likewise, conservative, evangelical religion, with its cooperative ventures in mission, social activism, and children's religious education found a welcome home in America. Revivals became an accepted form of religious expression. The long-standing domination of philosophy by confessional traditions was replaced by secular philosophy, which, though recently shaken, continues to assert its influence on American intellectual culture with its strong, historical grip of America's universities.

Antediluvian Americans, especially evangelicals, continued to raise questions about historical development, social, and more recently biological evolution; and the old rivalry between science and religion, while lately having shown signs of easing, has been rekindled by the attempt of the evangelical right to weave creationist theories of design

---

1. For years Nevin was, off-and-on, the acting president of the college. The board never managed to raise sufficient funds to cover his salary, and so he decided that he would not accept the position as permanent.

2. Historically, universalism is the doctrine that hell is a temporary punishment and that all intelligent beings will be saved at the end of time. However, the expansion of Unitarian Universalism is characterized by its emphasis on ethical issues and its embrace of scientific progress and rationalistic philosophy.

into biology. This recent controversy bears witness to the grip of dualism and the predilection of America's philosophic orientation. What dinosaur bones seemed to do to undermine faith in the nineteenth century, the big bang theory seemed to have reversed in the late twentieth century. Yet the subtle encouragement brought by the big bang theory might have tempted evangelicals toward a pseudoscience.

It has become habitual for twentieth- and twenty-first-century conservative Christians to expect that in order for both science and religion to be correct, they must somehow corroborate each other's findings. The much-talked-about and representative question of that continuing mind-set is as much a challenge as it is a question: What evidence could be supplied to falsify a religious claim?

After the brilliant and successful career of Philip Schaff, historians increasingly distanced themselves from ideological camps, applying the rigor of science in pursuit of objectivity. Inductive theology, the science of "proofs," and biblical criticism found prestige and legitimacy in their correspondence with rational inquiry. In effect, the principles inculcated in common-sense realism, as these principles would come to inform American pragmatism, seemed to "work" for just about everybody, especially for those Protestants primarily concerned with the nationwide cooperative ventures that captivated the country. The "Church Question," so important to Mercersburg, although momentarily trendy in the international High-Church movement (made famous by Oxford), never captured center stage, nor did the related questions of the sacraments, the importance of Christology, and the nature of ministry.

Ultramontanism[3] won its greatest battle in the *Syllabus of Errors* and the decree of papal infallibility in 1870, for decades dashing all hopes of Protestant and Roman Catholic dialogueue. Ecumenical ventures rarely led to union. Cooperation resulted from the practicality of banding together to achieve mutual goals, and in spite of widespread cooperation, America saw a proliferation of new religious denominations and sects. Fragmentation within Protestant denominations was rampant.

It would appear that Mercersburg's attempt to move America in an evangelical and catholic direction failed. In spite of their enormous

---

3. Ultramontanism in the nineteenth century was fueled by those within the Roman Catholic Church who were opposed to growing theological liberalism of the age. It is the movement favoring authority's being centralized in the papal Curia.

creative energy, Mercersburg came to realize that Americans, more and more, thought individually rather than collectively, and when they prospered in a collective consciousness, it was in terms of a practical pluralism and not a romantic idealism. Still, the lessons of Mercersburg had some lasting impact, especially in the South.

John Adger of South Carolina's Columbia Seminary was a close follower of the debate of Hodge and Nevin. He found Nevin's work fascinating, and it provided new life to his own presentation of Calvin's *Institutes of the Christian Religion*.[4]

Mercersburg made an even greater impact in the South through the efforts of W. P. DuBose, perhaps at the time the Episcopal Church's leading theologian. DuBose borrowed freely from the Mercersburg corpus, and his influence among Episcopalians was significant.

Finally, mention must be made of Charles Philip Krauth of the Lutheran Church. Krauth was a leading representative of the Lutheran High-Church movement of the nineteenth century, an articulate theologian, and a major influence among Protestants in America.

Still, Mercersburg's express wishes for American theology fell far short of the mark. Nineteenth-century America's adaptation of European practical philosophy wedded a justification for technological progress to the remarkable findings of experimental science. The resulting framework shaped the development of American institutions and traditions. In religion, Charles Hodge stands out as a supreme example of one who worked within this framework and welcomed the opportunity for advance brought by science.

Bacon, Reid, and Stewart were generally revered for the defense they brought to the way of life that was gaining wide acceptance among Western cultures. Inductive science was no threat to evangelical religion as long as theologians and scientists sustained dualism, as long as nature and revelation could peacefully coexist, and as long as experimental science restricted itself to the analysis of natural phenomena. Generally, scientists were satisfied to work exclusively within the sphere of nature. But as new fields of empirical inquiry opened up, scientific findings seemed to challenge traditional ideas, which understandably led to speculation beyond the findings themselves. Geology, paleontol-

---

4. E. Brooks Holifield provides an excellent study of this in "Mercersburg, Princeton, and the South," 238–58.

ogy, and anthropology strained what had been a cordial relationship. Tension arose especially around the question of creation.

More and more the separation of mind and body came under attack. But this time, not from those who would repair the ancient rift or argue that there is but one universe whose reality is both nature and spirit, but by those whose quest for empirical or factual evidence for religious claims led them to new questions about reality: Maybe there is only one universe. Maybe the only predicate is substance whose nature is matter. Maybe the unity of experience so celebrated by poetry and religious language is really the unity created by the wonderfully complex biochemical mechanism called the human brain. Maybe the "other world" is nothing more than the distorted image we get when we hold an ideological mirror up to nature.

Although Mercersburg did not seek to modify German idealism to suit American tastes, the idealism of Mercersburg had a regional flavor. Even Rauch participated in the adaptation by translating his speculative approach into the American idiom. Likewise, Schaff soon gained appreciation of the American context, and he was astute enough to understand that his efforts would be more effective if he adjusted them according to America's unique partition of religion and politics.[5] Finally, Nevin had specific issues that were distinctly American that preoccupied him. He brought the Mercersburg system to bear on these issues, and, so, added a further twist to the idealism sponsored by the German Reformed Church.

In his later debate with Isaac Dorner,[6] Nevin delved into the deepest depths of Christology and the mediating theology—so deep, indeed, that he lost the attention of those unable or unwilling to pen-

---

5. The classic example of this is Schaff's brilliant little book, *Church and State in the United States*. Schaff became one of America's most esteemed church historians and a renowned professor at Union Theological Seminary. His volumes on the *Creeds of Christendom* and the *History of the Christian Church* continue as vital reference works in academic study.

6. The controversy began with Dorner's criticism of Nevin in his "Der Liturgische Kampf in der Deutsch-Reformirten *Kirche von Nord-Americka*." It was published in the *Jahrbucher für deutsche Theologie* but appeared latter and poorly translated in the *Reformed Church Monthly* (run by the anti-Mercersburg forces) as "The Liturgical Conflict in the Reformed Church of North America" in 1868. Nevin already knew of Dorner's criticism and published throughout 1867 his reply. These articles appeared in the *Messenger* ("The Church Movement") and the *Mercersburg Review* ("Our Relations to Germany").

etrate the complexities of the concepts involved. But even here, Nevin was steeped in controversy. The debate with Dorner was sparked by accusations brought by the anti-Mercersburg faction of the German Reformed Church. Dorner turned on Nevin, thinking him an enemy; and while the debate was fascinating, it went far beyond the controversial issues that were demanding resolution.

Those questions remained the topic of debate even after Schaff and Nevin parted company, and the evangelical challenge hasn't changed a great deal over the decades. These basic issues reveal a deep-seated division in the way evangelical and liberal Christians view the world today. Again, Mercersburg cynically but succinctly listed the evangelical conclusions that rankled them, conclusions that remain informative for the host of modern evangelicals: revivals make Christians, do they not? Roman Catholics are papists steeped in superstition, are they not? Hegel and Schleiermacher were pantheists, or were Nevin and Schaff misquoted? Common-sense realism is simple, straightforward, and utterly compatible with the American temperament, or was the term "common sense" wrongly applied?

These were the questions, as much as the terms of debate, as they were outlined by Hodge and his supporters. It's not hard to appreciate Mercersburg's dilemma. These were certainly not the questions as far as they were concerned. Yet until their critics were satisfied as to Mercersburg's individual piety, as to their condemnation of Rome, as to their rejection of Hegel and Schleiermacher, and as to their commitment to plain speaking, there could be no progress in dialogue.

Of course, Mercersburg was quite clear that as far as they were concerned, piety is not a numbers-game; that "pseudo"-Protestants are reactionary Roman Catholics with a paper pope; that Hegel and Schleiermacher, with the biblical authors, would not bifurcate reality; and that realism is so simple as to be naive.

Obviously, with the two combatants unwilling to agree to the questions of debate, there was no progress in dialogue; and the Mercersburg movement, finding itself alone on an isolated ideological continent, drifted out of the mainstream of America religious life.

The Mercersburg movement may be extinct, but like those celebrated dinosaur bones that created such a stir so long ago, Mercersburg's legacy is impressive. The movement still arouses curiosity among the inquisitive, still attracts bright and articulate scholars and students, and still boasts descendents who survive in the form of the United Church of Christ "Mercersburg churches." In recent years, The *Mercersburg Review* has been resurrected, and a Mercersburg Society has been formed to promulgate the principles of the Mercersburg school. Gone, but of lasting memory, Mercersburg continues to exude intrigue, ferocity, and elegance. Its theological clarity, historical brilliance, and liturgical art are unsurpassed in American Protestant experience, and the legacy that remains is significant enough to hold the interest of any lover of fossils.

Bibliography

Albanese, Catherine L. *Sons of the Fathers: The Civil Religion of the American Revolution*. Philadelphia: Temple University Press, 1976.

Alexander, J. Addison. "Historical Theology." Review of *What Is Church History? A Vindication of the Idea of Historical Development*, by Philip Schaff. *Biblical Repertory and Princeton Review* 19 (1847) 91–113.

Alexander, James W. "Rauch's Psychology." Review of *Psychology; or a View of the Human Soul*, by Frederick A. Rauch. *Biblical Repertory and Princeton Review* 12 (1840) 405–9.

Alexander, James W., and A. B. Dod. Review of *Elements of Psychology, including a Critical Examination of Locke's Essay on the Human Understanding, with Additional Pieces* and *Introduction to the History of Philosophy*, by Victor Cousin and "An Address delivered before the Senior Class in Divinity College, Cambridge," by Ralph Waldo Emerson. *Biblical Repertory and Princeton Review* 11 (1839) 37–101.

Alhstrom, Sydney E. "The Scottish Philosophy and American Theology." *Church History* 24 (1955) 257–72.

Apple, Theodore. *The Life and Work of John Williamson Nevin*. Philadelphia: Reformed Church Publication House, 1889.

Augustine. "On True Religion." In Augustine: *Earlier Writings*, edited by J. H. S. Burleigh, 225–83. Philadelphia: Westminster, 1953.

Barbour, Ian G. *Myths, Models and Paradigms: A Comparative Study in Science and Religion*. New York: Harper & Row, 1974.

Berg, Joseph. "The German Controversy." *Protestant Quarterly Review* 3 (1846) 302–20.

———. "Mercersburg Theology." *Protestant Quarterly Review* 3 (1846) 75–87.

Bowen, Francis. Review of *Psychology; or, a view of the Human Soul*, by Frederick Rauch. *Christian Examiner* 30 (1841) 385–88.

Bozeman, Theodore Dwight. *Protestants in an Age of Science: The Baconian Ideal and Antebellum American Religious Thought*. Chapel Hill: University of North Carolina Press, 1977.

Calvin, John. *Institutes of the Christian Religion*. Edited by John T. McNeill. 2 vols. Philadelphia: Westminster, 1977.

Carlough, William L. "German Idealism and the Theology of John W. Nevin." *Reformed Review* 15.3 (1962) 37–45.

Crouter, Richard. "Hegel and Schleiermacher at Berlin: A Many Sided Debate." *Journal of the American Academy of Religion* 48 (1980) 19–43.

DeBie, Linden J. "Frederick Augustus Rauch: First American Hegelian." *The New Mercersburg Review* 19 (1996) 70–77.

---. "Real Presence or Real Absence? The Spoils of War in Nineteenth-Century American Eucharistic Controversy." *Pro Ecclesia* 4 (1995) 431–41.

---. Review of *Psychology; or, a View of the Human Soul*, by Frederick Augustus Rauch. *The Owl of Minerva* 16 (1984) 87–88.

---. "Saving Evangelical Catholicism for Today." *The New Mercersburg Review* 6 (1998) 11–20.

---. "Truce in the Dutch Crusade." *The New Mercersburg Review* 3 (1987) 17–22.

Easton, Lloyd D. *Hegel's First American Followers: The Ohio Hegelians*. Athens, OH: Ohio University Press, 1966.

Erb, William H. *Dr. Nevin's Theology: Based On Manuscript Class-Room Lectures*. Reading, PA: Beaver, 1913.

Forstman, Jack. *A Romantic Triangle: Schleiermacher and Early German Romanticism*. AAR Studies in Religion 13. Missoula, MT: Scholars, 1977.

Galbraith, John Kenneth. *The Age of Uncertainty*. Boston: Houghton Mifflin, 1977.

Gaustad, Edwin S. *Faith of Our Fathers: Religion and the New Nation*. San Francisco: Harper and Row, 1987.

Good, James I. *History of the Reformed Church in the U.S. in the Nineteenth Century*. New York: The Board of Publication of the Reformed Church in America, 1911.

Harpster, Donald E. "Controversy in the German Reformed Church in Pennsylvania With Emphasis On Nineteenth-Century Philadelphia." PhD diss., Pennsylvania State University, 1976.

Hegel, G. W. F. *The Difference between Fichte's and Schelling's System of Philosophy*. Translated by H. S. Harris and Walter Cerf. Albany: SUNY Press, 1977.

---. *The Phenomenology of Mind*. Translated by J. B. Baillie. New York: Harper & Row, 1967.

---. *The Philosophy of Right*. Translated by T. M. Knox. London: Oxford University Press, 1967.

Helfenstein, Jacob. "The Mercersburg Controversy." *The Weekly Messenger of the German Reformed Church* 2 (1846).

---. "The Rule of Faith." *Protestant Quarterly Review* 2 (1846) 119–31.

Hodge, Archibald Alexander. *The Life of Charles Hodge*. New York: Scribners, 1880.

Hodge, Charles. "Doctrine Of the Reformed Church, On the Lord's Supper." *The Biblical Repertory and Princeton Review* 20 (1848) 227–78.

---. "Idea of the Church." *Biblical Repertory and Princeton Review* 25 (1853) 249–90, 339–89.

---. "Nature of Man." *Biblical Repertory and Princeton Review* 37 (1865) 111–35.

---. "Princeton Review and Cousin's Philosophy." *Biblical Repertory and Princeton Review* 28 (1856).

---. "Schaf's [sic] Protestantism." Review of *Principle of Protestantism As Related to the Present State of the Church*, by Philip Schaf. *Biblical Repertory and Princeton Review* 17 (1845) 626–36.

---. Review of *Der Anglogermanismus, eine Rede u.s.w.*, by Philip Schaf. *Biblical Repertory and Princeton Review* 18 (1846) 482–83.

---. *Systematic Theology*. 3 vols. Peabody, MA: Hendrickson, 1999.

Hoeveler, David. *James McCosh and the Scottish Intellectual Tradition*. Princeton: Princeton University Press, 1981.

Holifield, E. Brooks. "Mercersburg, Princeton, and the South: The Sacramental Controversy in the Nineteenth Century." *Journal of Presbyterian History* 54 (1976) 238–58.

Johnson, Kathryn L. "The Mustard Seed and the Leaven: Philip Schaff's Confident View of Christian History." *Historical Magazine of the Protestant Episcopal Church* 50 (1981) 117–70.

Kant, Immanuel. *The Critique of Judgment*. Translated by James Creed Meredith. Oxford: Oxford University Press, 1952.

———. *Critique of Practical Reason*. Translated by Lewis White Beck. Indianapolis: Bobbs-Merrill, 1956.

———. *Critique of Pure Reason*. Translated by Norman Kemp Smith. New York: St. Martin's, 1965.

———. *Religion within the Limits of Reason Alone*. Translated by Theodore M. Green and Hoyt H. Hudson. New York: Harper & Row, 1960.

Lauer, Quentin. *Hegel's Concept of God*. Albany: SUNY Press, 1982.

Lewis, Taylor. "The Church Question." Review of *The Principle of Protestantism*, by Philip Schaff. *Biblical Repository* 2 (Third Series) No. 4 (1846) 79–137.

Locke, John. *An Essay Concerning Human Understanding*. Edited with an introduction and critical apparatus by Peter H. Nidditch. Clarendon edition of the Works of John Locke. Oxford: Clarendon, 1975.

Massey, Marilyn C. *Christ Unmasked: The Meaning of "The Life of Jesus" in German Politics*. Chapel Hill: University of North Carolina Press, 1983.

Miller, Eugene F. "Of scepticism with regard to the senses." In *Essays: Moral, Political and Literary* by David Hume. Indianapolis: Liberty Fund, 1985.

Mitchell, Nathan D. "Church, Eucharist, and Liturgical Reform at Mercersburg: 1843–1857." PhD diss., University of Notre Dame, 1978.

Mossner, Ernest C. "Introduction." In *A Treatise of Human Nature* by David Hume. Baltimore: Penguin, 1969.

Nevin, John W. "Answer to Professor Dorner." *Mercersburg Review* 15 (1868) 534–646.

———. *Antichrist: Or the Spirit of Sect and Schism*. New York: John S. Taylor, 1848.

———. *The Anxious Bench, Antichrist, and the Sermon Catholic Unity*. Edited by Augustine Thompson, OP. Eugene, OR: Wipf & Stock, 2000.

———. "Christianity and Humanity." *The Mercersburg Review* 20 (1873) 469–86.

———. "The Church Movement." *Reformed Church Messenger* 33:32, 37, and 41 (1868).

———. "Commencement Address." *Mercersburg Review* 14 (1867) 485–508.

———. "Cur Deus Homo." *Mercersburg Review* 3 (1851) 220–38.

———. "The Doctrine of the Reformed Church on the Lord's Supper." *Mercersburg Review* 2 (1850) 421–548.

———. "Dorner's History of Protestant Theology: Second Article." *Mercersburg Review* 15 (1868) 325–66.

———. "The Dutch Crusade." *Mercersburg Review* 6 (1854) 67–117.

———. "Early Christianity." *Mercersburg Review* 3 (1851) 461–90; 3 (1851) 513–62; 4 (1852) 1–54.

———. "Election Not Contrary to a Free Gospel." *Presbyterian Preacher* 1 & 2 (1832–1834) 209–24.

———. "'Human Freedom' and 'A Plea for Philosophy': Two Essays." In *Addresses and Essays by Schaff, Nevin and etc.* n.d. Reprinted in *The American Review* (1849) 9–10.

———. "Introduction to Schaff's *Principles of* Protestantism." Chambersburg: Publication Office of the German Reformed Church (1845) 3–27.

———. "Jesus and the Resurrection." *Mercersburg Review* 13 (1961) 169–90.

———. "Letter to the Rev. Dr. Harbaugh." Personal papers of Rev. Amos Seldomridge, 1872. Published in *Catholic and Reformed: Selected Writings by John W. Nevin*, edited by Charles Yrigoyen Jr. and George Bricker, 405–11. Pittsburgh Original Texts and Translation Series. Pittsburgh: Pickwick, 1978.

———. *My Own Life: The Earlier Years*. Papers of the Eastern Chapter, Historical Society of the Evangelical and Reformed Church 1 Lancaster, PA: Historical Society of the Evangelical and Reformed Church, 1964.

———. *The Mystical Presence: A Vindication of the Reformed Calvinistic Doctrine of the Holy Eucharist*. 1867. Reprint, Eugene, OR: Wipf & Stock, 2000.

———. "Our Relations to Germany." *Mercersburg Review* 14 (1867) 627–33.

———. "Party Spirit: An Address." In *Addresses and Essay of Schaff, Nevin and etc.* (Mercersburg, November 1953), Speer Library, Princeton Seminary, Princeton New Jersey, n.p., n.d.

———. "Philosophy of Dr. Rauch." *Biblical Repository* 10 (1843) 418–31.

———. "Pseudo-Protestantism." *Weekly Messenger of the German Reformed Church* 10.48–52 (1845).

———. Review of *Natural and the Supernatural, as together consisting the one system of God*, by Horace Bushnell. *The Mercersburg Review* 11 (1859) 176–77.

———. Review of Rauch's *Psychology*, by F. A. Rauch. *Weekly Messenger of the German Reformed Church* 5 (1840).

———. "Sacramental Religion." *Protestant Quarterly Review* 6 (1849) 129–40.

———. "Wilberforce on the Incarnation." *Mercersburg Review* 2 (1850) 164–96.

Nichols, James Hastings. *The Mercersburg Theology*. New York: Oxford University Press, 1966.

———. *Romanticism in American Theology*. Chicago: University of Chicago Press, 1961.

Nidditch, Peter H. "Foreword." In *An Essay Concerning Human Understanding* by John Locke, viii–ix. Clarendon edition of the Works of John Locke. Oxford: Clarendon, 1975.

Noll, Mark. "Evangelicals and Reformed: Two Streams, One Source." *The Reformed Journal* 31 (1983) 8–15.

———."What Has Wheaton to Do With Jerusalem: Lessons from Evangelicals for the Reformed." *The Reformed Journal* 32 (1983) 8–14.

———. *The Princeton Theology, 1812–1921: Scripture, Science, Theological Method from Archibald Alexander to Benjamin Breckinridge Warfield*. Grand Rapids: Baker, 1983.

———. *The Scandal of the Evangelical Mind*. Grand Rapids: Eerdmans, 1994.

O'Meara, Thomas F. *Romantic Idealism and Roman Catholicism: Schelling and the Theologians*. Notre Dame: University of Notre Dame Press, 1982.

Parker, T. H. L. *John Calvin: A Biography*. Philadelphia: Westminster, 1975.

Penzel, Klaus. "The Reformation Goes West: Development in the thought of Philip Schaff." *Journal of Religion* 62 (1982) 219–41.

Rauch, Frederick Augustus. "Every Man Is the Lord's." *Mercersburg Review* 11 (1859) 222–31.

———. "Faith and Reason." *Mercersburg Review* 8 (1856) 80–94.

———. "German Characteristics." *Weekly Messenger of the German Reformed Church* 1, New Series No. 30 (1836).

———. *The Inner Life of the Christian*. Philadelphia: Lindsay and Blakiston, 1856.

Reardon, Bernard M. G. *Religion in the Age of Romanticism: Studies in Early Nineteenth-Century Thought*. Cambridge: Cambridge University Press, 1985.

Reid, Thomas. *An Inquiry Into the Human Mind, On the Principles of Common Sense*, 1785. Reprint, Bristol: Thoemmes, 1990.

Rorty, Richard. *Philosophy and the Mirror of Nature*. Princeton, NJ: Princeton University Press, 1979.

———. Review of *Philosophical Papers*, vol. 3, *Realism and Reason*, by Hilary Putnam. *London Review of Books* 6 (1984) 6.

Ryan, J. P. "John Williamson Nevin: The Concept of Church Authority, 1844–1858." PhD diss., Marquette University, 1968.

Schaff, David. *The Life of Philip Schaff*. New York: Scribners, 1897.

Schaff, Phillip. *Christ and Christianity*. New York: Scribners, 1885.

———. *Church and State In the United States, or The American Idea of Religious Liberty and Its Practical Effect*. New York: Scribners, 1889.

———. "Princeton und Mercersburg." *Der Deutsche Kirchenfreund*. 1 (1848) 154–57.

———. *Theological Propaedeutic: A General Introduction to the Study of Theology, Exegetical, Historical, Systematic, and Practical, Including Encyclopedia, Methodology, and Bibliography*. New York: Christian Literature, 1892.

———. *The Person of Christ: The Perfection of His Humanity Viewed as a Proof of His Divinity*, 12th edition. New York: American Tract Society, 1882.

———. *The Principle of Protestantism*. Chambersburg: Publication Office of the German Reformed Church, 1845.

Schriver, George. "Passages in Friendship: John W. Nevin to Charles Hodge, 1872." *Journal of Presbyterian History* 58 (1980) 116–22.

———. "Philip Schaff's Concept of Organic Historiography: Interpreted in Relation to the Realization of an 'Evangelical Catholicism' within the Christian Community." PhD diss., Duke University, 1960.

———. "Philip Schaff: America's Destiny in the Unfinished Reformation." *Journal of Presbyterian History* 50 (1972) 148–59.

———. "Philip Schaff as a Teacher of Church History." *Journal of Presbyterian History* 47 (1969) 74–92.

Smith, Kemp. *A Commentary on Kant's "Critique of Pure Reason."* London: Macmillan, 1923.

Solomon, R. C. *In the Spirit of Hegel: A Study of G. W. F. Hegel's Phenomenology of Spirit*. New York: Oxford University Press, 1983.

Stansbury, Arthur J. *Trail of Albert Barnes, Before the Synod of Philadelphia*. New York: Van Nostrand & Dwight, 1836.

Stepelevich, Lawrence S. "Eucharistic Theory: Hegelianism and Mercersburg Theology." *The New Mercersburg Review* 22 (1996) 3–16.

Stout, Harry S. *The New England Soul: Preaching and Religious Culture in Colonial New England*. Oxford: Oxford University Press, 1986.

Trost, Theodore L. "Philip Schaff's Concept of the Church; with special reference to his role in the Mercersburg Movement." PhD diss., University of Edinburgh, 1958.

Ullmann, Carl. "The Distinctive Character of Christianity." *Theologische Studien und Kritiken*, 1845.

Witherspoon, John. *Lectures on Moral Philosophy*. Philadelphia: Woodward, 1822.

Woolverton, John. "Nineteenth-Century Ecclesiology: J. W. Nevin and the Episcopalians." *Historical Magazine of the Protestant Episcopal Church* 49.4 (1980) 361–87.

Yerkes, James. *The Christology of Hegel*. Albany: SUNY Press, 1983.

Yrigoyen, Charles Jr., and George Bricker, editors. *Catholic and Reformed: Selected Writings by John W. Nevin*. Pittsburgh Original Texts and Translation Series. Pittsburgh: Pickwick, 1978.

Ziegler, Howard J. B. *Frederick Augustus Rauch, American Hegelian*. Franklin and Marshall College Studies 8.Lancaster, PA: Franklin and Marshall College, 1953.